Vancouver Vice

Vancouver Vice

Crime and Spectacle in the City's West End

Aaron Chapman

ARSENAL
PULP PRESS
VANCOUVER

ARSENAL PULP PRESS
Suite 202 – 211 East Georgia St.
Vancouver, BC V6A 1Z6
Canada
arsenalpulp.com

The publisher gratefully acknowledges the support of the Canada Council for the Arts
and the British Columbia Arts Council for its publishing program, and the Government
of Canada, and the Government of British Columbia (through the Book Publishing Tax
Credit Program), for its publishing activities.

   Canada

Arsenal Pulp Press acknowledges the xʷməθkʷəy̓əm (Musqueam), Sḵwx̱wú7mesh (Squamish),
and səl̓ilwətaʔɬ (Tsleil-Waututh) Nations, custodians of the traditional, ancestral, and unceded
territories where our office is located. We pay respect to their histories, traditions, and
continuous living cultures and commit to accountability, respectful relations, and friendship.

Efforts have been made to locate copyright holders of source material wherever possible. The
publisher welcomes correspondence from any copyright holders of material used in this book
who have not been contacted.

Cover design by Jazmin Welch
Front cover image: CROWE Archives c/o Gordon Price
Back cover images (top to bottom): *Vancouver Sun*, February 17, 1961, 1; Glenn Baglo,
Vancouver Sun, 1977, c/o *Vancouver Sun* Archives; Ian Lindsay, *Vancouver Sun*, 1984,
c/o *Vancouver Sun* Archives; CROWE Archives c/o Gordon Price
Text design by Electra Design Group
Edited by Derek Fairbridge
Copyedited by Shirarose Wilensky
Proofread by Alison Strobel
Indexed by Catharine Chen

Printed and bound in Canada

Library and Archives Canada Cataloguing Publication:
Title: Vancouver vice : crime and spectacle in the city's West End / Aaron Chapman.
Names: Chapman, Aaron, 1971– author.
Description: Includes bibliographical references and index.
Identifiers: Canadiana (print) 20210226404 | Canadiana (ebook) 20210226455 |
    ISBN 9781551528694 (softcover) | ISBN 9781551528700 (HTML)
Subjects: LCSH: West End (Vancouver, B.C.) | LCSH: Crime—British Columbia—Vancouver
    —History—20th century. | LCSH: Vice control—British Columbia—Vancouver—
    History—20th century. | LCSH: West End (Vancouver, B.C.)—Social conditions—
    20th century. | LCSH: West End (Vancouver, B.C.)—History—20th century.
Classification: LCC HV6810.V3 C43 2021 | DDC 364.9711/33—dc23

Contents

Lost Lagoon in 2021.

Murder at Lost Lagoon

It was just before seven o'clock on the evening of Wednesday, May 2, 1984, when police and ambulance first arrived on a quiet, tree-lined stretch of road along the north side of Lost Lagoon in Vancouver's Stanley Park.

The weather forecast had predicted partly cloudy with a few showers, but so far the rain had held off. And even though North Lagoon Drive was shaded by a tall canopy of trees, with the forest of the great urban park behind it, there was still plenty of evening light. The late-spring sun wouldn't set for another hour or so.

A report of a suspected homicide had come from the Vancouver Police Department (VPD) communications centre at 312 Main Street. Details were sparse in the initial radio dispatch: Two men at the scene reported finding an abandoned car, a vehicle they said they recognized. They reported that the driver was missing. No mention of a body. It was unclear at the time how they knew the vehicle or the driver. Later, the police considered the possibility that the two had been trying to break into the car when they discovered a body in the trunk and had fabricated the story to cover their tracks. Even innocent people can make up an alibi when they get nervous and find themselves in the wrong place, at the wrong time.

As police from around downtown responded to reports of the abandoned car, some made derisive or even homophobic wisecracks that, given the proximity to the gay cruising areas along Stanley Park's Lees Trail, the driver would likely be back shortly with a pair of muddy knees, wondering why all the police had shown up. But when the details emerged that a body had been found in the trunk of the car, the joking stopped.

Police humour is a particularly dark brand of levity that others, who don't regularly deal with dead bodies, can often find macabre, or just plain insensitive. But police, firefighters, and paramedics often share this sardonic point of view among themselves as a coping mechanism to help them weather the often unrelenting stress of their jobs—especially if they've done the job for years. Even so, hardened veterans become solemn and put aside flippant jokes when they walk into a homicide scene in an area as public as Stanley Park—especially when there is a possibility that more than one victim might be discovered.

The car had been parked on a lay-by big enough for a vehicle to stop for a short time without interrupting traffic on the two-lane North Lagoon Drive. Trees and brush along the roadside gave the spot enough shade and cover to make it difficult to see who or what had parked there when viewed from the south side of the lagoon.

Ambulance attendants David Morris and Wayne Banks viewed the body upon arrival but did not disturb it. Two patrol constables, Les Yeo and Ray Winters, the first police to arrive, set up a perimeter to preserve the crime scene. They were followed by detectives Fred Johns and Ken Larkie from the VPD's Major Crime Section.

Any time a homicide is reported over police dispatch, it is always met with a significant initial response. Ambulance and homicide investigators arrive, but there are a host of others who report to such scenes—pathologists, forensics, a body disposal crew. Available uniformed patrol officers in the area also provide support, if for nothing more than crowd control when the crime scene is in a public place. On this particular call, a retinue of department officials arrived at Lost Lagoon, as well as some who, years later, would become well-known names in the Lower Mainland. Coroner Larry Campbell—mayor of Vancouver from 2002 to 2005 and inspiration for the TV series *Da Vinci's Inquest*—was present, as was a young District One patrol officer, Constable Bob Rich, just four years into his law enforcement career, who would become chief constable of the neighbouring city of Abbotsford in 2008. District One spread from Beatty Street, along the southeastern edge of downtown, to the end of Stanley Park, and included all of the West End and much of downtown but not the Downtown Eastside. District patrol supervisors Sergeant Brian Honeybourn and Corporal Phil Potts arrived on the Lost Lagoon scene, as did VPD fingerprint expert Sergeant Joe Mikita from the forensic identification unit to collect evidence.

Contemporary homicide investigations are markedly different from those in the 1980s. If the same homicide had occurred today, it probably would have led to the mobilization of an additional twenty police officers to cordon off the area and perform a ground search to comb for evidence forty to fifty feet back into the bush of Stanley Park. Today, forensic computer technicians with 3-D scanning technology are also regularly deployed to a crime scene to create

North Lagoon Drive in 2021.

simulations and maps, and the investigation results in enough boxes of reports, notes, photographs, interview transcripts, and documents to fill an entire storage room. But in 1984, aside from an immediate search of the area, a few photographs of the car and surrounding scene, some notes and diagrams, and a handful of interview transcripts, a 1980s homicide case often didn't fill much more than a single large legal-sized file folder.

In this particular situation, perhaps a greater search of the area simply wasn't considered necessary. Much of the immediate crime scene seemed to speak for itself. It was certainly clear the cause of death was not accidental, because of the blunt force trauma the victim sustained, and because they'd been shoved into the trunk of a car. And from the lack of blood around the scene of the vehicle, compared to what was isolated in the trunk, police suspected that this spot was not the original location of the murder.

Doctors from the VPD pathology department at the scene officially pronounced the victim dead and determined that the death appeared not to have occurred in recent hours but likely a day or two previous. The telltale odour of a body, dead for a while and stored in an enclosed space in warm weather, was certainly not unfamiliar to the veteran police officers present—one didn't need a university accredited forensic science background to recognize that smell.

Joggers and people on their evening stroll around Stanley Park began to stop along the police tape to get a closer look.

Some of the officers recognized the victim inside the trunk. Casual speculation had begun among them about this person who was "known to police." At this point, one more police officer arrived, walked up to the rear of the vehicle, and saw, unveiled from behind some bloodied blankets, the body of the victim. And that's when the rain that had been forecast for the day began to fall.

Staff Sergeant Rich Rollins from the Major Crime Section had marked his seventeenth anniversary with the Vancouver Police Department the day before. He would become the senior officer of this investigation. "I spent a lot of years on homicide investigations, and I saw a lot of autopsies," says Rollins, recalling that day in May, almost forty years later. "This ended up being one of the most interesting cases I ever worked, and just when I thought it couldn't get more bizarre, it did."

INTRODUCTION

The Davie Street Blues

Thirty-two years after that body was found in Stanley Park, there would be another very different kind of unveiling. It would seem completely disconnected from that incident in May 1984. This one took place at the corner of Jervis and Pendrell Streets in front of St. Paul's Anglican Church—just a five-minute drive from Lost Lagoon—where the West End Sex Workers Memorial, a black Victorian-style lamppost crowned by a red lamp, was presented to the public on September 16, 2016. On this day, former West End sex workers along with city officials, members of the police, media, and many local residents gathered to witness this subdued event.

Lately, the monument's vintage glass globe has looked like it could use a bit of polishing. The bulb now seems to glow a dusky pink at night rather than the vibrant crimson of the red-light district beacon it is meant to symbolize. As a simple street lamp along the sidewalk, the memorial is an inconspicuous part of the surrounding streetscape, so much so that a rushed passerby probably would not take notice of the four inscriptions on the base of the post: DEDICATED TO A DIVERSE COMMUNITY OF SEX WORKERS; IN MEMORY OF THEIR ONGOING STRUGGLES FOR EQUALITY; PEOPLE WHO LIVED AND WORKED HERE FROM MID-1960s–1984; and TODAY, WE COMMEMORATE AND HONOUR THEIR LIVES.

Newer residents of the West End can be forgiven if they are unaware of the history behind those inscriptions. As time passes, fewer and fewer residents who lived through the late 1970s and early '80s remain to recount stories from the neighbourhood. Denizens from that era have moved out, passed away, or, in more recent years, been priced out of this expensive real estate zone. Others still may have simply chosen to forget. And beyond the boundaries of the West End, with so many new arrivals to Vancouver expanding the population of the city, there are many who have little to no knowledge of the neighbourhood's tumultuous recent history.

Although the West End Sex Workers Memorial honours those it recognizes, the plaques alone do not fully explain the turmoil of this era. The significance of those years certainly isn't immediately evident to someone on a stroll through the streets of the West End today. The look of the neighbourhood hasn't changed much. Newer, taller condo towers now crowd the skyline, but many of the older apartment buildings, constructed during a development boom in the late 1950s and '60s, remain. Many side streets in the West End feel somewhat like a time capsule—like this orderly residential area has been this way for decades.

The holdovers from those earlier days of the West End are even more noticeable to those who drive up and down its grid where a number of curbs extend awkwardly—almost quaintly—into intersections and mini courtyard parklets in front of walk-up apartment buildings block streets and prevent cars from proceeding. These traffic-calming measures can easily leave drivers who are unfamiliar with the area confused and frustrated as to why so many streets are seemingly inaccessible. Meanwhile, these diversions also provide safe, unharried shortcuts through the neighbourhood for pedestrians and cyclists. Indeed, these directional quirks have been in place long enough that most residents seldom stop and think about why they were put there in the first place. Newer West Enders might be surprised to learn that these detours were installed forty years ago to discourage motorists in search of a pickup from cruising alongside sidewalks in the area filled with what was once counted to be between 200 and 300 sex workers of any gender, 40 to 50 of whom might be working on any given day or night.

It was a dramatic time of both fear and hope, guilt and innocence, perhaps unlike any that Vancouver had seen before or has experienced since. Although many citizens and some of the local media felt that police and municipal administrators had lost control of the West End, others celebrated the personal—particularly sexual—freedom that was deemed permissible here. For many of the area's residents, it was also a time of growing social unity—an exciting moment that saw the emergence of new liberties. It was also a time of conflict, because the city's more socially conservative ruling class was opposed to this cultural revolution. Although conventional wisdom recognizes the 1960s as the decade of social change, in Vancouver it was in the 1970s that many of these changes started to take hold. But this was also an era marred by scandals, scams, and swindles.

By the late 1960s, curious suburban Vancouverites were known to pile into the family car and head west to Kitsilano and, like gawking tourists on safari, drive along West 4th Avenue to see the new countercultural phenomenon, the hippies who occupied that then-affordable neighbourhood. In the following couple of decades, those same vicarious thrill-seekers would drive to the West End to gape at the sex workers (or "hookers" in the parlance of the time) congregated along the streets. Local TV news reports increasingly featured stories about the conflict between West End residents and sex workers, complete with lurid nighttime footage of anonymous legs in high-heeled boots walking street corners and leaning into driver's-side windows. Those stories, coupled with images of the flamboyant outfits and exuberant celebrations at gay pride parades running along Denman Street, led many reserved, conservative households throughout the Lower Mainland to perceive the West End as a kind of modern-day Sodom and Gomorrah—a free-for-all of pushers, perverts, and pinkos.

Public opinion of police dimmed as residents complained that the city had merely stood by and allowed street prostitution to take over *their* neighbourhood, unchecked. On the other side, sex workers complained that they were being unfairly harassed by police and bullied by neighbourhood vigilante groups. They also argued that law enforcement officials were less concerned about *their* safety.

Further decades later, even the seemingly harmless West End Sex Workers Memorial managed to open some old wounds upon its unveiling. Supporters of the memorial felt it honoured those who once worked those streets before they were shamed and shooed away from the neighbourhood and into more dangerous locations. The sex workers themselves saw it as a monument to an often safer, more equitable period for their trade, an era less dominated by pimps and exploitation, when workers observed cooperative practices, working in pairs, sharing bad-date lists and writing down licence plate numbers from the cars of customers. Some workers, like Jamie Lee Hamilton, a former sex worker and in later years a neighbourhood activist who championed the creation of the memorial, opined that the "open brothel culture" that developed provided an economic benefit to the neighbourhood itself.

Other residents balked at memorialization, particularly in letters to the editor in local newspapers and phone-in talk radio shows, positing that the lamp was merely a reminder of days when johns prowled the neighbourhood in search of pickups, and women were unable to walk city streets without being propositioned—something these residents thought should not be celebrated. A small but vocal minority even suggested in an online petition the memorial should be removed.

Beyond the upheaval regarding the downtown sex trade, there were other significant social changes occurring in the West End during the 1970s. Vancouver's gay community, which had long called the West End its home, was gaining broader recognition and some acceptance across the city. This was long before rainbow crosswalks appeared on Davie Street, when many gay residents practised extreme discretion regarding their personal lives to avoid being alienated by friends, family, or co-workers. The risks of being "out" ran from awkward social encounters to life-threatening gay bashing. Yet in the West End, gay individuals drew strength and support from this growing community.

The 1970s also saw the expansion of the city's gay nightspots, even though the venues often didn't outright advertise themselves as such. The various bars, nightclubs, and steam baths provided discreet spaces for drinking, dancing, and sexual encounters, where customers could forget their worries—and each other's names—all before the dark spectre of AIDS.

Paradoxically, the gay community was taking its pioneering steps toward liberation in an era when Vancouver was arguably at its most socially conservative as a city. The public tussle over morality played out across the city, with everything from no alcohol on Sundays to grassroots anti-pornography campaigns to exotic dancers charged with obscenity to crackdowns on adult film theatres and gay bathhouses and raids on magazine stores that sold material that city authorities considered objectionable. City council members sought to outlaw public nudity at Wreck Beach. And they marched in protest outside a Granville Street cinema, suggesting that buying tickets to see the sexually explicit historical drama *Caligula* would also surely guarantee moviegoers good seats in hell.

If Vancouver was going to hell, though, which door led to it depended on who you asked. During the 1980s, Canada Border Services Agency seized books that were deemed "obscene material" from the legendary West End queer bookstore Little Sister's. This occurred at the same time as the dawn of the robber baron era of Vancouver's financial district, when all manner of stock pump-and-dumps took place, and secret deals ran so wild that *Forbes* magazine would eventually describe the Vancouver Stock Exchange as "the scam capital of the world."[1]

---

[1] Joe Queenan, "Scam Capital of the World," *Forbes*, May 29, 1989.

Perhaps too much is made in retrospect in the popular history of the West End of the battle over street sex work as the single most important social and legal issue in the community in the 1970s and '80s. The area also experienced higher crime rates overall. For years, the large number of crimes from bank robberies to muggings remained high. It was an era when there was not one but two incidents of snipers shooting at police on Davie Street. Worst of all were the homicides. In 1982, Vancouver police revealed that more murders had occurred in the West End than in the Downtown Eastside, a neighbourhood widely considered to be the city's most crime ridden. Yet, although the headlines and crime statistics were of concern, the West End continued to be publicly perceived as an unassuming residential community filled with locally owned stores, safe schools, socially engaged parents, and nurtured children. Perhaps this criminal activity wasn't particularly remarkable at the time because Vancouver, as a whole, was experiencing an increase in crimes like nothing it had seen before, from the serial killer murders of Clifford Olson to the anarchist activist bombings of Direct Action—better known as the Squamish Five. There was also local political upheaval and labour unrest—a beer strike by unionized brewery workers in 1980 that created beer shortages, a three-month strike by garbage collection workers in 1981 that resulted in angry residents dumping their trash at the front door of city hall, and the Solidarity labour protests of 1983 against the provincial government that saw 60,000 demonstrators form the largest single protest in BC history. It was as if Vancouver had decided to sow as much of its wild oats as fast as it could—exorcise all of its urban demons—before the city got together for the family photo of Expo 86, the world exposition that would transform and define the city for the years that followed. Perhaps development and gentrification would remove from the portrait these oddball cousins and wayward uncles that the city hoped to forget.

But the story in *Vancouver Vice* is not told to review how one neighbourhood went to war with itself but to explore a wider history of the West End by telling the stories of those on both sides of the law. Too many in this chapter of the city's history have passed on before their time, unable to tell their own story. Many seem to have vanished from memory; others will never been forgotten. And while some former sex workers who once walked the streets of the West End celebrate an era that they feel was less compromised by exploitation, there are others whose experiences were not as fortunate. But they, too, speak on the record, in newspaper articles, police reports, and interviews with those who knew them as friends—or enemies. Many are now speaking, here in this book, for the first time about those years. Decades later, they feel freer to open up. Some even gave their interviews before passing, prior to the completion of this book.

This book is not a meant to be simply a sampling of the police blotter of West End crime, or a complete history of the vice squad, but a story of how, for a time, Vancouver dealt with its vices—drugs, alcohol, illegal gambling, pornography, and prostitution—some of which no longer attract the same degree of police attention. It was a turbulent time, the likes of which the city will probably never experience again. Even the VPD vice squad no longer exists under that title.

But there is one element that runs through all the years of this story: the idea that geography is destiny. The city itself—its neighbourhoods, its communities—plays its own distinct role in this story.

For all of the city's verdant beauty, so often revered especially by outsiders, there is another side to Vancouver: a city of temptation, secrets, and darkness. And it is in this part of Vancouver where so many individuals in this story lived, worked, suffered, prospered, and even died. And it is in this Vancouver where a series of events came to a head on North Lagoon Drive on May 2, 1984, in a way that would reveal a nexus of crimes and conflicts, the full story of which has never been told until now. But that story, and that Vancouver, doesn't begin at the shores of Lost Lagoon but with the rise of the West End itself.

CHAPTER 1

Electricity and Sex

For decades, Vancouver's West End has been one of the most recognizable areas in the city. Perhaps most familiar from postcard-worthy photos, taken regularly from the beach across English Bay at Spanish Banks when the tide is out, presenting downtown Vancouver as a shining modern citadel. On a clear day the West End skyline, with tree-lined beaches in front and the Coast Mountain range towering in the distance, presents a striking visual testimonial in natural beauty for why Vancouver is repeatedly voted one of the most desirable places in the world to live. And the West End neighbourhood is often celebrated as one of its most popular residential communities in the city.

Any history of the West End often begins with the near mythological story of the Three Greenhorns: John Morton, Samuel Brighouse, and William Hailstone, the first non-Indigenous settlers in the area. In 1862, the trio purchased 540 acres —180 acres each—of land, which now represents the entirety of the West End, for $550.75 from the colonial government. Observers at the time thought the three men were foolhardy. Other European settlers felt that a dollar an acre was an overpayment for what was fundamentally a remote, worthless chunk of land, clogged with trees, scrub, and bracken. The plot was more than twenty kilometres away from New Westminster, then the major population centre of the Lower Mainland—a considerable distance to travel in a region without proper roads.

The Greenhorns would eventually be redeemed in 1886, when the Canadian Pacific Railway (CPR) made its way to the town of Granville—later to be named Vancouver. CPR officials who knew of development plans for the area bought up lots that the Greenhorns owned and in the process ended up making the West End the town's first upscale neighbourhood.

That the Greenhorns had to wait nearly twenty years, which included ponderous road-clearing efforts, before their investment paid off hardly makes for the kind of get-rich-quick real estate story that has been promulgated in local lore. The story of how the Greenhorns "settled" the area later named the West End also ignores the fact that Indigenous people had been living on this land for 3,000 years or more. As late as the 1930s, Squamish Nation Chief August Jack Khatsahlano, who was born in 1867, could still remember and delineate the locations of villages and settlements he had known as a child when the Squamish people migrated to Burrard Inlet in the summer to gather food for the winter—a concept that perhaps should give pause to the many Vancouverites today who grouse about how much the city has changed in their own lifetime.

But early histories of the West End, whether from the Indigenous or settler perspective, do not shed much light upon how the modern West End developed into the community that we recognize today, or what factors drove it to such tumult in the 1970s. Although rapid postwar growth in Vancouver might be seen as an obvious cause, less recognized are the influences of sex and electricity—not necessarily in that order.

In the 1890s, the first streetcars started to run in Vancouver, and by 1900, they extended down both Granville and Davie Streets. Initially, there were plans for the streetcars to be pulled by horses, until city planners saw the future in the electric trams. The cars ran down Robson, Denman, and Davie Streets, essentially framing the borders of the West End with Granville Street, leaving no area resident farther than three blocks away from public transportation. Trolley buses and eventually modern city buses ended up using the same routes and largely the same stops.

Davie Street remains the community's main thoroughfare—its backbone. Running roughly two kilometres from False Creek to English Bay, the road leads through the heart of the West End. At its northwestern end, near the intersection of Davie and Denman, palm trees can be seen in and around the streets surrounding Morton Park. A warm sea breeze coming in off the water on a nice day can make this small wedge of Vancouver seem more Californian, perhaps, than British Columbian.

While the electricity of its public transportation system defined the outline of the West End, its unique homes and citizens filled in its character. As more working-class families moved into the neighbourhood around the turn of the twentieth century, the West End's wealthier residents began to migrate uptown to Shaughnessy, leaving behind hundreds of Edwardian-style wooden homes—

1700 block of Davie Street in July 1958. The West End building boom in the 1960s changed the West End forever. Between 1959 and 1972, developers built more than 220 high-rise apartment buildings.

grand houses with bay windows and large verandas, some even featuring a corner turret with a conical roof. Although they were not built for this purpose, they were ideal structures to be transformed into multi-occupant rooming houses. By 1910, there were 400 rental suites in the district. Throughout the 1920s and into the late 1940s, the West End remained an affordable neighbourhood for middle- and lower-income residents. By the 1950s, the city's new zoning laws led to the construction of more walk-up apartment buildings. While the Marpole and Kerrisdale neighbourhoods also saw considerable apartment building development during this time, no area in Vancouver was transformed as much as the West End as more and more three-to-six-storey walk-ups took the place of the old rooming houses.

This development ushered in a new kind of West End resident. "West End Starts Unique Comeback," trumpeted a front-page story in the March 30, 1953, edition of the *Vancouver Sun*. The article noted, "The sort of person who now lives in the West End apartment area is neat, often smart, respectable, solvent, without being rich. He or she likes the type of furniture, radio, television set, curtains, and so on that one gets in a good department store."[2] If the word "yuppy" had existed in 1950, the West End might have been thought as the new natural habitat for them.

Not that all residents were so easily convinced. The cynical complaints often heard around dinner tables and at coffee shops ranged from *How could one sleep next door to people you don't know?* to *There are no front yards!* Traditionalists felt that such development had ruined the old West End and was ruining the city where they'd grown up. Objections from that time are strikingly similar to those made by some contemporary Vancouverites who deride the modern condominium towers that have sprouted up over the last twenty years, leaving them to remark that the once-despised old walk-ups of the 1950s and '60s are now beacons of city heritage and sustainable living.

In turn, in order to attract a modern, younger clientele, developers in the 1950s and '60s gave their buildings names suggestive of cosmopolitan sophistication, like the hip New Yorker on Broughton Street, or the cool jazz San Franciscan vibe of the Golden Gates Apartments on Comox. Building names were often hand-painted in black-and-gold cursive lettering on glass entrance doors, many of which can still be admired today.

The Pacific breeze that wafted into the West End from English Bay would curve paths around new buildings that would pop up in the coming years. The West End apartment boom was under way. Buildings sprang up on blocks that just a year before had comprised only old single-family homes. The 1960s saw 17,000 new apartment suites built in Vancouver, mostly in the West End. By 1971, more than ninety-seven percent of dwellings in the West End were apartments.[3]

High-rises were the next big change in the West End. In a thirteen-year run, from 1959 to 1972, developers built more than 220 high-rise apartment buildings, several of them more than twenty storeys.[4] These new towering apartment complexes provided convenient housing for the ever-expanding workforce as jobs proliferated in the growing downtown corporate sector. A flood of secretaries, salespeople, flight attendants, nightclub performers, and hairdressers began to populate the neighbourhood. There was a marked difference between

[2] "West End Starts Unique Comeback," *Vancouver Sun*, March 30, 1953, P1.
[3] Bruce Macdonald, *Vancouver: A Visual History* (Vancouver: Talonbooks, 1992).
[4] Chuck Davis, *The Greater Vancouver Book: An Urban Encyclopedia* (Surrey, BC: Linkman Press, 1997).

these new residents and the seniors and immigrants that had long been part of the community.

None of the architects who designed these towers would probably have imagined it, but the high-rises filled with a new kind of modern Vancouverite: the swinging single. Thousands of young, professional, single West Enders now mixed everywhere from the laundry room to the beach to the bedroom. And helping to grease the wheels of this burgeoning social activity, the city granted its first cocktail lounge licences in 1968. Downtown apartment dwellers who didn't want to stay home on a Saturday night could socialize at nearby clubs and chic new watering holes. Now hundreds of unattached young people with no parents around to intervene had elevator access to each other and to a vibrant nightlife within walking distance. It was a remarkable social sea change: casual sex was now a topic for open discussion when, just ten years earlier, Lucy and Ricky couldn't be seen sharing a bed together on TV.

And while the society pages of the local mainstream media focused most of its attention on how men and women in the West End were enjoying this new-found sophisticated urban freedom, Vancouver's gay community was along for the ride, too.

In many larger cities across North America, especially since the liberation of the 1969 Stonewall uprising protests in response to a police raid on the Stonewall Inn, a well-known gay bar in New York City, particular neighbourhoods developed into distinct and prominent gay communities: San Francisco had the Castro District, New York City had Greenwich Village, Toronto had Church and Wellesley. Vancouver was no exception. But how exactly the West End became the home to much of the city's gay population isn't as clear.

There is an urban creation myth that Alexander Davie, British Columbia's premier from 1887 from 1889, was gay, and that Davie Street and Davie Village became the epicentre of the city's gay community as a kind of tribute to a pioneering queer, but there isn't much historical evidence to support this. The true origin story probably doesn't go back that far in time. The genesis of the community is often more officially connected to the social liberation movements of the early 1970s, but many Vancouverites of a certain age today recall Davie Street and the surrounding West End as being the gay neighbourhood in the 1950s and even earlier.

Homosexuality was decriminalized in Canada in 1971. That this occurred so recently makes it difficult to parse the often-vague historical record to determine how Vancouver's local gay community grew out of the secrecy of those decades *before* 1971. There wasn't much positive media coverage of the gay community —local or otherwise—during these years when homosexuality was widely considered to be deviant behaviour.

However, most local historians agree that the anonymity of high-density living and the affordability of bachelor suites for "confirmed bachelors" in the neighbourhood's early rooming houses and apartment suites made the West End an appealing and convenient location for gay men as far back as the 1920s.

By the 1960s, the West End saw the arrival of a new generation of young gay men as residents. The private apartments provided "places where they could be themselves with one another before it became visible," says Ron Dutton, archivist and founder of the BC Gay and Lesbian Archives, which as of 2018 are in the permanent collection of the City of Vancouver Archives. "That was the lifesaver for most people of that generation. Much of that happened in the West End because you could have an apartment party and nobody was going to blink an eye or notice that there's an awful lot of men there and not many women."[5]

At this time there were no real public spaces downtown that could be considered welcoming or accepting where men could be openly gay. Some places like the bar at the Hotel Vancouver, the Castle Hotel pub on Granville Street, or some outdoor locations around English Bay were unofficially considered low-key "friendly" social spaces, but gay people were still perceived, at least by the conventional wisdom of mainstream media, as mentally ill people indulging in a dark and dangerous lifestyle.

In 1959, three murders occurred in the West End, collectively referred to as the Bachelor Murders. In each case, the media referred to the victims as "bachelors," and implied that their identities as gay men were contributing factors in their murders. In January of that year, fifty-seven-year-old Eddie Beresford, a waiter at the Vancouver Club, was murdered in his apartment at 980 Jervis Street by a pair of assailants, aged twenty-seven and fifteen. The two were originally found guilty of murder and sentenced to hang, but in court appeals they had their convictions reduced to mere robbery charges. In June, Charles Chatten was the victim of an axe slaying in his apartment at 1450 West Georgia Street. Although police detained a suspect in the case, who was later deported, the murder remains unsolved to this day.

But it's the March 1959 "bachelor murder" of forty-three-year-old Robert White that stands out as the most glaring instance of a victim being blamed

5 Ron Dutton quoted in "Davie Street Village," *Places That Matter*, Vancouver Heritage Foundation, n.d., placesthatmatter.ca/location/davie-street-village/ (accessed September 5, 2021).

for his own murder because of his sexual orientation. White, a bartender at the Arctic Club on West Pender Street, had met a stocky, scruffy-haired, thirty-seven-year-old Romanian merchant sailor named Konstantin Dumitru who was on shore leave from a freighter in Vancouver's harbour. White was enjoying a drink at the club on his night off when he and Dumitru struck up conversation. At closing time, White invited Dumitru back to his apartment at 1209 Jervis Street for more drinks. Dumitru later claimed that once at White's apartment, White came onto him aggressively, and in defending himself, Dumitru choked White with a shirt sleeve. After a twenty-minute struggle, White was dead, and Dumitru fled the apartment and returned to the freighter. The subsequent VPD investigation resulted in police only catching up with Dumitru when his freighter was in Hawaii—where he was then extradited by US Marshals back to Vancouver.

Bartender Slain in West End Suite

Victim Found Dead Of Strangulation

A 43-year-old city bartender was found murdered Saturday in his neat West End apartment.

Police identified the man as Robert White, of suite 109, Blenheim Court, 1209 Jervis.

His husky, five-foot-seven inch body was found sprawled on his living room rug, a white shirt knotted lightly around the neck.

Police said White, a widower, died late Thursday or early Friday morning.

Loud banging sounds, heard by White's neighbors shortly before midnight Thursday, led police to believe that White put up a violent struggle for his life although the apartment showed signs of only a "slight scuffle."

An autopsy showed White suffered two large bumps on his head before he died of strangulation.

The bumps, said coroner Glen McDonald, "might or might not have been enough to knock him out."

White had been employed at the Arctic Club for four years.

NO MOTIVE FOUND

Police have found no motive for the attack but believe White might have invited the killer into his apartment.

Friends, neighbors and fellow-workers all described the murder victim as a man of high morale, quiet, easy-going and well-liked.

A veteran police official said White could have met an acquaintance while returning home Thursday and invited the man into the apartment for a drink.

White's neighbors, Mrs. Noreen May, suite 176, and Robert Johnson ... ... coming from White's apartment.

Constable R. R. Gemmell smashed open the door after he and Stiles looked through White's living room window and saw the body.

Police, tracing White's last movements, found he was off from his regular job Thursday, but spent the afternoon tending bar at the Pacific National Exhibition for the Motorama show's preview cocktail party.

An inquest has been tentatively set for 10:30 a.m. Tuesday.

ROBERT WHITE
...murder victim

BOB FORTUNE

Along with the forecast's quota of gloom this week, there is a lot of talk about backing and veering winds.

The words backing and veering, as applied to wind, are as old as tea.

Because few of us are anything approaching that old we should hardly be expected to know how the words are used. Both words, used this way, belonged originally to the seamen and have only slipped into land usage in the ... wind backing to east or west, wind backing to south southeast, etc.

A veering wind is just the opposite. A veering wind changes direction clockwise—usually experienced as storm passes through.

Southeasterly winds are expected to veer to southwesterly ...

The murder of Arctic Club bartender Robert White at his Jervis Street home was just one of three West End "Bachelor Murders" in 1959.

For weeks, Vancouverites followed with fascination daily newspaper accounts of the subsequent trial. Dumitru, defended by lawyer Harry Rankin, later a Vancouver city councillor, claimed that he'd been the victim of a "homosexual attack." This was a classic "gay panic" defence—a legal strategy whereby defendants claimed they were so offended or frightened by an unwanted same-sex sexual advance, that they committed assault, or murder, as a justifiable act of self-defence.

The jury not only found Dumitru not guilty of murder but, despite Dumitru being in possession of White's wristwatch at the time of his arrest, not guilty of murder during the commission of a robbery. It left Dumitru to be convicted only on the lesser charge of manslaughter, with a sentence of three years in jail. Dumitru only served fifteen weeks before he was deported on an immigration technicality back to Europe, where he lived freely for the rest of his life.

The incidence of serious crimes like these in the West End remained relatively low, despite the rise in population density, but the area did experience its fair share of drug issues. Nickel-and-dime narcotics busts were an everyday occurrence in the Downtown Eastside, but it was in the West End that cops were nailing the bigger traffickers. An increasing number of drug dealers called the West End home during the 1960s residential boom. Just prior to Christmas 1965, Vancouver police raided the Comox Street home of thirty-eight-year-old Robert Gentles and seized $24,000 worth of heroin. Gentles had not had an easy life. One of the survivors of the Granduc Mine disaster in northern BC near the Alaska Panhandle earlier that year that claimed the lives of twenty-eight miners, he had twenty-three convictions, including drug-trafficking offences, going back to 1947. He had been in league with a retired New Westminster doctor and a Burnaby waitress to traffic the heroin when police had made the arrests, but his lengthy list of priors landed him the biggest sentence—fifteen years in prison.

Just a few months later, on May 5, 1966, Vancouver police and Royal Canadian Mounted Police (RCMP) drug squad officers raided the Lincoln Arms apartment building at 1306 Haro Street, the home of twenty-nine-year-old Larry Anders. Police found two revolvers, an empty bank money bag, and more than 120 LSD capsules. Sources stated that Anders was the "Kingpin of LSD" in Vancouver, where he met buyers between the library stacks of the old Vancouver Public Library building at Robson and Burrard. He was sentenced to three months in jail and a $500 fine, and in the process became the first person in Canada to be charged and convicted for selling the hallucinogen.

By 1968, the West End, which had about eight percent of Vancouver's population, was experiencing forty-two percent of the city's apartment break-ins and eighteen percent of its car thefts. Yet for twenty-one hours out of every twenty-four, only six police officers at a time were on duty to handle what was then a population of more than 35,000.[6]

Elderly residents in particular voiced concerns about what was perceived as an increase in criminal activity in the West End. Seventy-eight-year-old Ena Davidson, who had been born in 1888 in Vancouver and lived most of her life in the West End, told the *Vancouver Sun* in a 1966 interview about her memories over

[6] Stan Shillington, "High Rise Area Hard to Police," *Vancouver Sun*, September 20, 1968, 27.

The front page of the *Vancouver Sun* on September 17, 1969, that featured the stabbing death of twenty-six-year-old nurse Myrna Inglis.

the decades. She recalled the city when she was a high-schooler as "rambunctious" and noted that the even the Wild West pioneer days were not as tumultuous as they were in the 1960s: "All the bars were regular saloons, and there was a lot of fighting and drinking. It wasn't like it is now though, with all the muggings and so on."

"There's more crime in the West End than on Skid Road," said Roger Patillo, a research associate with United Community Services in a 1969 interview on the rise in crime that had seemingly come with the development in the community that supposedly made it more lucrative for thieves and criminals. "The highest number of breaking-and-entering complaints in Vancouver comes from the West End. Prostitution, drugs, thefts, all flourish." Patillo then noted the much-quoted statistic of that time: that the West End had become one of the most densely populated areas in North America, and only cities like New York and Chicago had areas of higher density.

But if there was one incident that galvanized fears about neighbourhood safety in the West End, it was the 1969 murder of Myrna Inglis. A twenty-six-year-old nurse, Inglis had been stabbed five times in the back and neck while walking home along the 1400 block of Nelson Street after her shift at St. Paul's Hospital. Two weeks later, another woman was stabbed by a suspect not believed to be connect to the Inglis killing. In the wake of these incidents, women in the city took to walking home at night in pairs or groups for safety, and many took self-defence lessons. No culprit was caught in either case, and Inglis's murder remains unsolved more than fifty years later.

As newsmaking as some of these incidents were, it could still be argued that, though troubling, they were relatively isolated. West Enders were put on guard but not thrown into community-wide panic. The neighbourhood was still largely considered to be quiet and comfortable. It's difficult to imagine that anybody would have predicted how much the West End would change by the mid-1970s. The result: a decade that was perhaps the wildest the modern city had ever seen.

CHAPTER 2

Vice and the Tumbling Dice

"It's tough to get men for the vice squad," said Inspector Ken Brown, who oversaw the VPD vice squad in the 1970s. "It's not the most pleasant of duties in the department. So when they do come, they're usually exceptionally good—*they* know what they're coming into and *you*, in command, know what you're getting. Trouble is they're of a certain quality and they tend to get promoted and usually at a time when they're your most experienced sources."

Perhaps Brown was simply being complimentary of those under him in his department at the time, but that abundance of riches hadn't always been the case. Historically, the vice squad had for years seemed to be at the heart of repeated and long-standing corruption within the VPD.

Sex work in Vancouver was almost as old as the town itself. It wasn't until 1916 that the VPD formed its first Morality Squad—a unit staffed by women. The VPD had been the first police department in Canada to hire women police officers. The task of the Morality Squad was mostly to handle sex-work cases and juvenile offenders. By 1924, under the leadership of Chief H.W. Long, the VPD had created a singular section of the department dedicated to handling drugs, liquor, gambling, and sex work.

The first head of this new squad was Inspector John Jackson, a veteran of nearly thirty years on the force. But Jackson, along with other members of the VPD, came under the scrutiny of the 1928 Lennie Commission on police corruption. An investigation exposed that although the vice squad performed some token arrests, it largely turned a blind eye toward open gambling, bawdy house operations, and bootlegging managed by the city's biggest organized crime figures. The Lennie Commission noted that although on some occasions junior members of the vice squad initiated investigations against criminals like Chinatown gambling

SUSPENDED DETECTIVES SUMMONED

Police Board Will Examine Vice Squad Officers On Saturday.

FOUR Vancouver detectives who were suspended for fourteen days by the Police Commission on Monday will appear before the board at a private meeting at 10 a.m. Saturday to answer questions regarding alleged vice conditions in the city.

Those who will face the commission enquiry are Sergeant R. S. Quirk, head of the morality squad; Sergeant George Sunstrum, of the liquor branch, and Detectives D.

The VPD vice squad were regularly plagued with accusations of corruption in the 1920s and '30s.

kingpin Shu Moy or pimp Joe Celona and his east end brothels, these investigations were eventually halted by senior department officials nearly every time. Even worse: along with VPD brass, then-mayor L.D. Taylor had been known to socialize with the city's underworld figures. These cozy relationships between the city authorities and the underbelly ran top-down, as the Lennie inquiries revealed that Moy had even held a private banquet in Inspector Jackson's honour.

This would hardly be the only scandal to tarnish the squad. In 1931, after a department-wide housecleaning following the Lennie Commission, Detective Sergeant George McLaughlin, who had been made the new head of vice a year earlier, and had resigned under pressure when his name came up in an investigation, was quietly rehired. When news of the reappointment reached the police commission, the resulting turmoil and blowback led to the resignation of the new Chief Constable W.J. Bingham. The circus continued in 1935, when Mayor Gerry McGeer—newly elected on his strong anti-crime platform—ousted Chief Constable John Cameron, along with seventeen other VPD officers.

When McGeer returned as mayor in 1947, he again took up the fight against police corruption, but this time with less success. A new round of officers dismissed over corruption and "inefficiency" charges were later found to be innocent and then rehired after the police union challenged their terminations. An even bigger misfire followed a few years later. In 1955, Walter Mulligan, McGeer's appointee for chief constable, became the highest-ranking member of the VPD to be deposed when he was found to be at the centre of a local corruption scandal that involved bribery payouts from two crime syndicates who paid police thousands of dollars for monthly protection of their gambling operations. Mulligan fled to California, and in the subsequent years, the VPD adopted a complete overhaul of its procedures and infrastructures—everything from training to uniforms.

The ostensible objective of the VPD vice squad was probably influenced by the prevailing attitude toward "vices" among the more privileged citizens of

Vancouver. The temperance movement of the late nineteenth century that later widened into a campaign against gambling and prostitution was largely a middle- and upper-class preoccupation. The working-class origins of most of the officers in the Vancouver Police Department in those years meant that they probably had more empathy for those less entitled citizens who were simply buying rum after hours from a bootlegger or playing the numbers or visiting brothels.

At the time the Vancouver police had also been dealt two significant budget cuts to a force that was already earning significantly less than their counterparts in other jurisdictions. Simple policies, such as officers not getting paid for testifying in court on their days off, became for some a possible disincentive to arrest criminals and lay charges. Catherine Rose observes in the book *Vancouver Confidential* that it became "easy to see how—individually and collectively and at all levels—the police could have justified the systematic harvesting of bribes."[7]

Gambling continued to be an enduring problem for the vice squad long after Mulligan left town, and it was no longer restricted to Chinatown and east end backrooms. In 1959, thirty-seven-year-old Jiri Stukl was arrested along with sixteen other card players at a gambling house that he had run at 618 Davie Street. Stukl was already known to police, having been arrested for heroin trafficking in 1957, and a few months earlier for the robbery of a West End apartment.

In 1961, twenty-six-year-old Donald Harris was charged with conspiracy to defraud and possession of a gambling device when the vice squad raided his Davie Street hotel room and found 500 pairs of loaded dice. Harris, along with two accomplices, used the dice to bilk a visiting Calgary man out of more than $17,000 in a crooked craps game. The dice, marked with Nevada casino branding, had hidden metal inserts that, when rolled with two powerful magnets hidden under the table activated by Harris, could force a dice roll to crap out or yield winning combinations of seven or eleven.

By the 1970s, the old days of the neighbourhood cigar-store bookie from the 1950s were long over. Police estimated there were forty to fifty well-established bookies in Vancouver throughout that decade, with another twenty scattered around the suburbs. They ranged from relatively big operators with connections to international syndicates to ramshackle, two-bit players who just wanted to make a living without having to work at it.

---

[7] Catherine Rose, "Street Kings: The Dirty '30s and Vancouver's Unholy Trinity," in *Vancouver Confidential*, ed. John Belshaw (Vancouver: Anvil Press, 2014), 149.

At the top end, there were those like Andre Ouellette who, while still in his thirties, rose to become perhaps the most prominent bookie in Vancouver in the 1970s, with connections to Montreal organized crime. Ouellette lived in a West End apartment on Beach Avenue but bounced between nightspots—from the Dover Arms on Denman Street to the Living Room nightclub on Hornby—to run his bookmaking operation. Ouellette was arrested multiple times between the mid-1970s and into the '80s but could afford to pay whatever fines he was given. The fines during this period were significant. In 1977, Vancouver bookmaker Donald Kolot was hit with the largest-ever fine at the time laid on a bookmaker in the city: $6,000. Kolot's list of criminal offences stretched back to the late 1950s. He had escaped from jail in Edmonton in the 1960s and was arrested in Texas before ending up in Vancouver, where he would continue his criminal ventures. By the time of his record-breaking fine, Kolot, with an estimated weekly gross of $50,000, was able to absorb the blow. After lying low for a period, he got back into the business of bookmaking.

The majority of those in Vancouver's illegal bookmaking trade in the 1970s were not criminal masterminds. They were often oddball, chain-smoking middle-aged men in checkerboard slacks with multiple ex-wives to support. For them, bookmaking was a natural evolution from the heavy gambling they did themselves. "Muffler Mel" Bateman was one of these guys. A low-level Vancouver bookie who owned a half dozen Midas Muffler outlets around the city, Bateman took bets over the phone from his home or from behind his desk at one of his auto shops. He was a convivial sort who sought mutually beneficial relationships with the police, often providing free service on the personal vehicles of VPD officers. He even took bets from police. His racket was horse racing.

"You have to remember at the time there wasn't any off-track betting," recalls retired detective Grant MacDonald, who joined the VPD in the mid-1960s. "You had to be there at the racetrack to make a bet, so sometimes bookies were just considered convenient if you couldn't make it out to the track." MacDonald explained that although larger bets made at bigger American thoroughbred raceways wouldn't alter the odds because of the number of bettors at a small track like Hastings Racecourse (called Exhibition Park in the 1970s), a larger bet or two could swing the odds from a long shot to a favourite. Some bettors used the unofficial bookies just for better odds. "There were any number of small bookies around during those days and I think the only damage they did was to the local racetrack," MacDonald suggests.

American National Football League (NFL) games drew the most gambling action in the city in the 1970s. The Coordinated Law Enforcement Unit (CLEU) in Vancouver confirmed that the NFL was big business, with an estimated $100 million a year in bets handled by British Columbia bookmakers. Almost all of these bookies were connected to stateside gambling, legal in Nevada but illegal in other parts of the country that were connected to organized crime. Prosecution of local bookies could be difficult, requiring many hours of investigation, often only resulting in arrests and convictions of very brief jail sentences, if at all. And most even moderately successful bookies could absorb the impact of fines with a good weekend of NFL bets.

Gambling was also facilitated in illegal after-hours booze cans run out of private homes. In the 1970s, Paul Dixon, then a Vancouver taxi driver in his twenties, recalls two prominent West End after-hours spots of that period. "In 1973 and '74, there were a couple of big old houses—one in the 1200 block of Comox and the other in the 1400 Barclay—that were straight out *The Sting*. The first time I was dispatched to the one on Comox, I pulled up at about four in the morning to this big old *Addams Family*–style house that was in total darkness." Unsure, Dixon called his dispatcher to check the address. He was told to go knock on the door. The home was completely silent. He climbed the steps with trepidation, and then knocked on the front door.

"The 'look-see' on the door popped open," Dixon says. "Oh boy, there was most definitely a party going on in there. I got the hairy eyeball, but when I said 'Taxi,' the eyeball said, 'Right out,' and they were indeed out directly. They must have had some sort of hallway 'airlock' inside, 'cause when the passengers came out the front door, there was no burst of light or noise at all."

Dixon says an older cabbie told him about the Barclay Street house, where "you had to know someone who knew someone" to get invited to a regular poker game. "One night at the Barclay spot, he realized he was being cheated out of his money," Dixon says of the other cabbie. "He voiced his objection, and the next thing he knew he was waking up in the back lane a block away with a very large lump on his head and a splitting headache that lasted a week."

Dixon suggests that the West End nightspots took particular care not to attract attention to themselves. They kept the noise down, both inside and out, and took care of cab drivers who came and went from them. "If by some chance a call resulted in a 'no load'—where a fare was a no-show or had decided to stay—the fella at the door gave you a couple of bucks."

The West End booze cans of the 1970s were a carry-over from the 1950s, when after-hours clubs operated along Granville Street, particularly along the 1000 and 1100 blocks. These clubs specialized in keeping a low profile. They were often operated in second-floor hotel rooms or apartment buildings, with sex workers on the floor above. Many hotels and rooming houses along Granville had hourly rates, and the desk clerk would only have to account for one booking in a twenty-four-hour cycle. The buildings themselves further concealed their backroom activities from police since alleyway entrances could only be accessed by a stairway. "Those stairways going up were always a good way to slow police down from charging in or trying to kick in the alley door," recalled the late Jack Ivers, a rounder and thief in the 1960s and '70s in Vancouver.

Tom Urchenko, who joined the VPD in 1955, today at age ninety-two recalls working in plainclothes detail with the dry squad, tasked with seizing alcohol in unlicensed clubs and cabarets. "In those days, I'd go around trying to find some of the after-hours places. So I'd go out at night, after places closed, asking where you could get a drink, or work my way out to get invited to them. Later, I'd meet the liquor squad guys in vice in Stanley Park in the middle of the night—brief them about where I'd been and what I'd seen, and they'd give me some money to buy drinks in these places. I did so much of that, I got sick of it and stopped drinking!"

Back in those days, when liquor stores were closed at night, or for entire Sundays, thirsty Vancouverites could reliably get a bottle from a hotel night clerk, as well as from taxi drivers who had contact with bootleggers who often had private stock in their homes and garages. But cabbies took a risk whenever they helped a fare procure a bottle, chancing a run-in with undercover members of the vice squad. "I was warned by a couple more experienced drivers to be leery about folks looking to score a bottle. Sunday nights after dark you might hear a comment over the radio about the 'dry squad' being out," Dixon says. "Sure enough, drive past the cab stand in front of the Blackstone Hotel [on Granville Street], and there'd be a couple of undercover police right out of central casting ... They'd get into your cab and start giving you a song and dance about being thirsty. It was just a matter of asking eventually if there was actually somewhere they wanted to go, and if not, then kindly get out. It was the same thing with the 'I need a girl' fares."

Many of the crimes that police dealt with in the 1970s—gambling, drugs, and bootlegging—are approached differently today. The days of sports bookies running a network of illegal gambling are largely gone. Today, the British Columbia Lottery Corporation runs Sports Action—allowing those who wish to place bets on winners, point spreads, and over/unders in sports games to do so directly with the government. Retired police officers who spent time on the drug squad in the 1970s could never have imaged the well-lit cannabis stores that now thrive openly in neighbourhoods across the Lower Mainland. And terms like "harm reduction" and "safe-injection site" would have seemed completely alien to police forty years ago. Although a couple of the old dial-a-bottle services still exist for those who remain thirsty after the bars have closed, there's really no profit to be made by a professional bootlegger anymore. But the Vancouver vice squad would continue to wrestle with aspects of the illegal sex trade for decades after the 1970s.

CHAPTER 3

Call Girls and Boys

It's a common misconception that sex workers didn't come to the West End until the late 1970s. But sex work has been taking place here—at least behind closed doors—as far back as the 1930s, when more than twenty bawdy houses were associated with criminal complaints during that decade. These establishments were largely shut down by the 1940s, but by then the "working girls" more commonly plied their trade in an assortment of downtown nightclubs, dance halls, and hotel lounges. Just about any bartender, bellhop, or cab driver in the city in those days knew where to steer out-of-towners, or for that matter lonely locals, who were looking for company. Many of these local "matchmakers," in fact, were paid commissions if they brought in new clients, a trend that continued through the 1950s.

On Thursday, November 10, 1960, the VPD vice squad led by Inspector Ian McGregor and Detective Sergeant Percy McCardell raided what police dubbed "the city's biggest call girl ring" and arrested eight women who had operated out of a West End apartment in Steven Manor at 1451 Burnaby Street. The raid was the result of a nearly year-long investigation by McGregor and McCardell, who had both joined the police department toward the end of the 1930s. McGregor had made a name for himself in a number of vice squad gambling investigations during the 1950s, and McCardell had received four commendations over his career.

Police noted that this particular business was highly organized. A dispatcher would use coded messages between the sex workers and their hotel outcalls. The operation was also very lucrative, pulling in $10,000 a month. Police not only charged the women with prostitution, which carried a maximum sentence of ten years, but also added conspiracy charges, similar to those pressed in cases of organized crime—the first time such charges had been laid in connection with a call girl investigation in Canada.

The ringleader of the operation had been a brothel madam in the city for years: thirty-five-year-old titian-haired Diane Frew. Although the fiery redhead

West End madam Diane Frew was the Vancouver sex scandal of 1961.

had listed her occupation in court as "housewife," Frew had a criminal record that stretched back two decades. She had been involved in running what crime beat reporters called plush set-ups in West End apartments used exclusively for prostitution since 1946.

Frew made local headlines in 1952 when she was arrested for living off the avails of prostitution. Police also came into possession of her black book, which contained the names of about 300 clients, some of whom, rumour had it, were among the city's most well-known gentlemen. The names were never published. Frew was sent to jail for three months and, though she was ordered to leave town upon release, went right back to work afterward with a new round of employees.

Frew made front-page news in the city again in 1961 after the raid led by McGregor and McCardell. Frew's little black book, now updated, was again a subject of interest, and again, the names therein were never mentioned in court or released to the public. What was reported were the names, ages, occupations, and even home addresses of women in Frew's employ. They ranged in age from twenty-one to twenty-four, many declaring such occupations as homemaker, waitress, and nightclub hostess. All provided details about the circumstances that had led them to sex work. Some had difficulty finding other work. Others, who were young widows, said they undertook the work to provide for their families. Only one confessed to working to support a drug habit.

Publishing personal details in the press might seem to be both prejudicial and an invasion of privacy today, but this was a standard approach to crime and court reporting during the period—an approach that continued well into the 1970s. Readers relished the scandalous mechanics of how Frew ran her business. Workers charged $25 for a "brief appointment" and $100 a night (one customer paid $3,500 over a sixteen-day period). Court testimony revealed that the women working for Frew gave her fifty percent of their earnings. Frew said she used that significant take of the earnings to maintain the business, phone lines, and operators, and to pay off the referrals from the hotel workers and taxi drivers who sent clients her way.

The service used three different phone lines managed by operators twenty-four hours a day. The *Vancouver Sun* even went so far as to publish the phone numbers, one of which was accidentally misprinted, resulting in the owner of that wrong number receiving a deluge of phone calls from all manner of curiosity seekers, pranksters, and heavy breathers. The newspaper was forced to print a correction in the following days.

All eight of the women in the Frew operation pleaded guilty. Frew was sentenced to nine months in jail, while her employees received sentences ranging from two to six months. After receiving their punishment, the women, including Frew, never appeared in Vancouver police arrest blotters again. It's unclear if they quit the trade afterward or felt that they had been so much in the public eye that they left town to begin again elsewhere with more anonymity.

Another West End sex work kingpin who cut an almost stereotypical figure of a pimp was Bobby Lee Cooper. In March 1973, twenty-five-year-old Cooper was convicted and sentenced to three years for living off the avails of prostitution. An American, Cooper lived in a West End penthouse apartment and drove a gold Cadillac. His prostitution ring was barely that; he had two women working for him, one of whom had earned at least $24,000 over the course of the previous year—a substantial amount of which Cooper took for himself. In passing sentence, the judge told Cooper he was a "pimp and procurer" at the bottom rung of society, and that he only considered a heroin trafficker lower. After serving his jail sentence, Cooper was deported back to the US.

The closure of downtown Vancouver's Penthouse Nightclub after a police raid in 1975 is often cited as a cause of the growth of street sex work in the West End. Since the 1950s, the Seymour Street nightclub had a reputation as an establishment frequented by sex workers—a de facto red-light district unto itself. It had been dubbed by a *Vancouver Sun* reporter of the time as a "union shop for hookers." By the 1970s, as many as 100 sex workers a night had come to use the nightclub as a working venue—a convenient and safe place to meet customers. "You could pretty much see the ruts that ran like streetcar tracks in the road from the Penthouse to a couple of West End apartment buildings, or to hotels where the tricks were staying," recalls taxi driver Paul Dixon.

The Penthouse had a well-earned reputation in the city as a popular nightspot for visiting entertainers, rounders, news reporters, and local show business people. The larger-than-life Filippone brothers, who ran the club, were veterans of Vancouver's entertainment scene, bringing everyone from Louis Armstrong to Sammy Davis Jr. to town to perform. They also had a long history of flouting liquor laws, and an equally extensive accumulation of fines for bootlegging. The Filippones didn't profit directly from sex work. They simply realized that having these women around was good for the nightclub's bottom line. Sex workers, along with other patrons, had to pay a cover charge to enter the club. So the additional traffic's impact on the club's revenue made it worthwhile for the Filippones to look the other way. However, with the appointment of new chief constable Don Winterton in 1974, and new vice squad head Inspector Vic Lake, both of whom vowed to confront downtown prostitution head-on, the Penthouse's carefree days were numbered.

In the summer of 1975, patrons of sex workers were photographed coming in and out of the nightclub by undercover police hiding in a camper van across the street. Following a raid that December, the Penthouse was shut down, forcing a bitter three-year court battle that the Filippone brothers finally won on appeal. But in more recent years it's been widely asserted in criminology and local history circles that during those three years the club was shuttered, sex workers were pushed out onto the streets of the West End and ultimately marginalized to other, less safe neighbourhoods. Many police of the era agree. "As far as I was concerned, the Penthouse was never a problem," says retired detective Grant MacDonald, who started his career in law enforcement as a West End beat cop and later became a homicide detective. "Everyone knew what was going on there. But it was controlled there. After the trial, the hookers poured out into the streets all over the city, including to areas that were already dealing with it, but it really became like trying to capture quicksilver to manage it again."

One of those areas was the West End, which now hosted not only the women who fled the Penthouse but also a growing number of cross-dressing male sex workers. For years police had regularly found male sex workers dressed as women, and occasionally trans women sex workers, along parts of Granville Street, or near Main and Keefer Streets, just outside of Chinatown. By the early 1970s, this was the case along the 1100 to 1300 blocks of Davie Street as well.

In an October 1971 story entitled "Pretty Men with Sex for Sale Have an Out in Criminal Code," *Vancouver Sun* reporter Lisa Hobbs noted a rising number of cross-dressing men working in Vancouver, with as many as "100 transvestite prostitutes who streetwalk," many passing so convincingly as women that their customers didn't realize they were male. Hobbs noted that many of the residents and police officers she spoke to didn't care what happened behind the closed doors of West End apartments where sex workers lived or worked out of, but that the activity had become so prevalent on West End streets at night that it was becoming a problem for the community as a whole. Hobbs's article captured the kind of near-hysterical fear common among many residents of the era, noting that West End sex workers were "turning a residential area into an extension of a cheapside bar, where you don't care for your teenage sons to wander, where Dad can't go to the corner grocery without factoring the obscenities of a male tart." Hobbs characterized one cross-dressing sex worker named John, who worked under the name Diane, as someone who "stops automobiles, bargains openly over a price, and accosts any adult pedestrian male who might prove to be a customer." Diane, wrote Hobbs, represented "a disturbing element of real perversity."

Hobbs writes nothing of the extreme prejudice faced by those in the cross-dressing and trans communities—even in the otherwise socially progressive West End—that left many marginalized and with few safe options for employment.

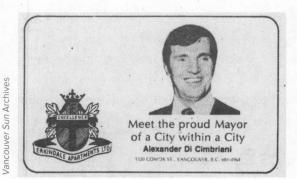

Meet the proud Mayor
of a City within a City
Alexander Di Cimbriani
1320 COMOX ST., VANCOUVER, B.C. 681-4964

Alexander DiCimbriani proclaimed himself the mayor of the "city within a city" and took out newspaper advertisements about himself. But DiCimbriani was not who he appeared to be.

Regardless of the impact the Penthouse's closure had on street sex work in the West End, the neighbourhood was experiencing massive change by the mid-1970s. A community that had developed twice as fast as the rest of the city was dealing with more than its fair share of growing pains.

In August 1974, thirty-three-year-old Serge Jean Leroux was found stabbed to death in a West End lane—another shocking West End crime that would go unsolved. Police made their usual appeal to the public for information, but with an additional incentive: Alex DiCimbriani, a neighbourhood millionaire and self-proclaimed "Mayor of the West End," offered $10,000 to anyone who could provide information leading to an arrest.

The kind of character that only Vancouver in the 1970s could produce, DiCimbriani was actually from Ontario. He arrived in 1960 and soon began dabbling in real estate, buying old rooming houses (back in the days when a labourer and maintenance man could afford to do so) and, rather than demolish them, renovating them. His efforts provided needed affordable housing for pensioners and low-income families. By 1967, he had become the landlord of 330 suites and 100 bachelor apartments, with the *Province* newspaper lauding him as an "enterprising renovator who turns West End potential slums into apartments for a wide range of incomes," particularly around the "Comox, Jervis, Broughton, Barclay area."

DiCimbriani's life story had all the dramatic highlights of a latter-day Horatio Alger tale. The story went that he was born near Toronto and raised by nuns in an orphanage. He later would say that no one adopted him because of a speech impediment caused by his cleft palate. One day, at the age of eight, he was caught stealing an apple from a grocery store by a local policeman who would become his only friend. He said that the police officer had faith in him and secretly paid for an operation for his cleft palate. DiCimbriani said he never forgot the gesture.

By 1974, at the age of thirty-two, he'd risen through the ranks of Vancouver's social and political set. His property acquisitions had made him a millionaire, and he became a big donor to the Social Credit Party that dominated provincial politics during the latter half of the twentieth century. He made public displays of his influence: he designed his own crest, Erkindale—the name of his apartment complexes—and wore it monogrammed on his blazers. He shelled out $25,000 to host a retirement party at the Bayshore Hotel for Vancouver police chief constable John Fisk. He was also a financial benefactor for a variety of West End cultural events. DiCimbriani began to boast to the press that the "Mayor of the West End" (a winking, honorary title that bestowed no power) would run for the actual office of mayor of Vancouver in the next civic election.

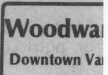

$20,000 REWARD SET IN WEST END KILLING

Rewards totalling $20,000 have been posted for information leading to arrest and conviction of the killer of Serge Jean Leroux, who was found stabbed to death in a West End lane earlier this month.

The Vancouver Police Board decided Thursday to match a reward offer of $10,000 from millionaire landlord Alex DiCimbriana.

Leroux, 33, was stabbed 18 times in a violent struggle with a mugger Aug. 3. His body was found lying face down near some bushes in the 1300 block Burnaby.

In other business, Chief Constable Don Winterton told the board in a report that extra policing on the Granville Mall has lowered the number of drug addicts in the area.

He said strongarmings near Victory Square have also dropped after 20 arrests were made by four policeman specially assigned to the area.

However, Winterton reported an over-all 5.8-per-cent increase in major crimes to July 31, compared with the same period in 1973. Heaviest increases are found in sexual offences, up 17.3 per cent; assaults, up 24.1 per cent; theft over $200, up 32.8 per cent, and possession of stolen goods, up 23.3 per cent.

Weapons and drug offences are up 16.3 per cent and 15.4 per cent, respectively.

He announced that the city will save about $200,000 a year when the provincial government takes over training of recruits from the Vancouver Police Academy.

Woodwa
Downtown Va

In August 1974, "millionaire landlord" Alexander DiCimbriani matched a $10,000 reward for an arrest leading to conviction for a West End murder that is still unsolved today.

It's difficult to pinpoint when things went sour for Alex DiCimbriani, but his glittering public image began to deteriorate in the mid-1970s as media investigations—particularly in the *Vancouver Sun* columns of Allan Fotheringham—dug into DiCimbriani's past and revealed he was not who he said he was.

As it turns out, upon arriving in Vancouver he'd changed his name from Ralph Sims. He was not an orphan. In fact, he'd been brought up as part of a large family in Hamilton. A series of complaints revealed that he was not the enterprising businessman who looked out for the little guy. Rather, he was a hostile landlord who'd had a number of physical altercations with his tenants over the years and once even evicted an elderly woman unable to pay her rent during a hospital stay. While the reward he offered for Leroux's murder was still up for grabs, DiCimbriani's political dreams were dashed overnight. The Mayor of the West End never fully recovered.

In the 1990s, DiCimbriani pled guilty to defrauding more than fifty investors, including many of his old Social Credit Party cronies, notably Premier Bill Vander Zalm, and eight VPD officers. The dark final blow to his reputation came when he was found guilty of sex crimes involving three teenaged boys, aged fourteen to sixteen at the time of the offences, and sentenced to a year in jail. Alex DiCimbriani, or Ralph Sims, or whoever he was, died in 1999. The $10,000 reward he'd offered twenty-five years prior was never claimed, and the murder of Serge Jean Leroux was never solved.

In 1969, a study of West End residents prepared by the city's Department of Social Planning and Community Development and the United Community Services of the Greater Vancouver Area perhaps best illustrated the changes under way in the neighbourhood. The area was home to 45,000 people, which was ten percent of the entire population of Vancouver—making it the most densely populated neighbourhood in Canada at the time. But the idealized, carefree beachside lifestyle that residents visualized in the 1960s had begun to dissipate by the mid-1970s. The report suggested that many of the neighbourhood's residents were increasingly concerned about crime rates. Senior residents said that they felt increasingly alone in this community. And while there were still plenty of young bachelors populating the West End, there were now much more single women—and they, too, described feeling loneliness in apartment living. Meanwhile, many of the marriages between people living in the West End did not survive. The report noted that fifty percent of West End schoolchildren were from single-parent families—with that parent employed full time. Implying a connection, the report noted that "25% of secondary school children had behavioural and emotional problems" that required special counselling services. The study showed that "only a small minority feels the West End is a desirable place to raise children."

For those growing up in the West End during this period, the advantages and disadvantages of the neighbourhood didn't go unnoticed. CBC Radio producer and journalist Pamela Post grew up in the West End during the 1970s, first attending Lord Roberts Elementary and later King George Secondary School.

She still calls the West End home today. "It was a wonderful neighbourhood to grow up in," Post says. "A real community of renters. I took it for granted, that 'hip, swinging' element of the West End back then. A lot of European immigrants, and a real mix of ages, many of whom were still living in the old rooming houses. But there was a seedy element, too."

Post recalls that the local schools experienced the problems common in other inner-city schools. "King George felt like a dumping ground for bad teachers," says Post, adding that it was easy for students to skip school unnoticed with so many single parents working. Even for those students who might have had good teachers or no family issues at home, Post recalls that the nearby destinations of English Bay and Stanley Park made for easy distractions. "It wasn't much different from East Vancouver in that way," she suggests. "I think a lot of the kids were loved, but there was a feeling we weren't necessarily as looked after or as protected as other kids in other neighbourhoods."

Post observes, "We hung out on Denman Street a lot back then. It felt safe—it still does to me. I never saw any prostitutes on Denman. But Davie Street felt different then—and as a teenage girl in the 1970s, there was a feeling of danger on the street, and that there were predators around."

CHAPTER 4

Down the Toilet

In September 1976, Constable Al Robson and his partner Constable Gordon Bader were in an unmarked police car parked near the intersection of Davie and Denman Streets doing surveillance on what seemed like an unlikely location—a public toilet. But just how they both found themselves there, and how that location came to police attention, is a story unto itself.

Born in Vancouver in 1942, Bader joined the Vancouver Police Department in 1971 as a patrol officer in District One. Today, long since retired, he is soft-spoken as he recounts stories of his years on the force in a relaxed but practical manner. Yet he recalls how eager he was when he first joined. During that era before field trainers were assigned to new recruits, the usual police orientation process was to pair a rookie with an older officer—a veteran who could impart some wisdom. It was not uncommon in those days for veterans either to tell the rookies to completely disregard what they'd learned in the police academy or to tell them nothing at all. In Bader's case, he simply wasn't seeing any action on the job. "My old partner was a bit of an anchor," Bader says with a laugh. "None of the old guys back then who were close to retirement really wanted to actually get out there and walk the beat, and I was just really eager to be more active on the street."

After a year on the job, Bader was itching for something more substantial. He was put on a plainclothes nightclub detail where "you'd go in and have a drink, looking to get information, or if you saw certain people meeting with others you'd make a note of it." But Bader's straight-and-narrow personality didn't serve him well in cases where he needed to glad-hand bar managers like Marty Roitman at Club Zanzibar or the Filippone brothers at the Penthouse Nightclub. High rollers like these would push free booze on those they knew were police and ensure that club strippers were seated with them. Often it seemed like club proprietors were trying to glean inside information from the police rather than the other way around.

Bader's first experience with the vice squad was on a gambling raid at Iaci's, a legendary Seymour Street restaurant, directly across from the Penthouse Nightclub. The Iaci family was related to the Filippone brothers. These two establishments, along with the nearby Emilio's Spaghetti House, made that block of Seymour Street in the 1970s rival Commercial Drive's claim to being Vancouver's Little Italy.

Unlike the Penthouse, Iaci's wasn't regarded as a gambling hub. It was known for having some of the best Italian food in town. It was operated in an old three-storey residential home where dinners were seated in the living room, or right in the kitchen in a booth that had been specially installed. There were no menus; patrons were served whatever the cooks—usually the Iaci sisters or their mother—had whipped up that night.

"The vice squad had run a [telephone surveillance] wire on the place for a month and found there was someone in the family there running bookmaking operation," Bader remembers. "Horse betting, sports betting, that kind of thing. The night of the raid, the front door behind their glass screen door had been locked, so we used an eighteen-pound sledgehammer to break it open. I had a hold on the door, but when I let it go and it broke open, I cut my thumb very badly and was bleeding all over the place."

Police started looking for evidence of the gambling operation but only found a couple of betting slips—nothing to corroborate what police believed had been occurring, and certainly not enough to support a charge.

"I saw this coffee table they had that looked odd to me," Bader says. "It was a regular-sized table, but it was several inches thick. There was this decorative saw cut around the edge of it, and I started grasping around, and the table started to part a little bit. But my bleeding hand prevented me from giving it a closer look, so I went to get it treated. One of the other guys got to the table eventually and was able to pull out a drawer, and out came hundreds and hundreds of betting slips. I was only miffed that when it was all over he got the credit for finding the slips, and all I got for it was a badly cut thumb. Iaci's is long gone now, but I always think I left a good chunk of my thumb there."

While Bader was busting open doors on Seymour Street, Al Robson had been making a variety of dramatic arrests in Gastown. Robson was born in Saskatchewan and raised in East Vancouver. He joined the VPD at age twenty-four, in 1971, just prior to Bader. Robson's father was already a twenty-plus-year veteran of the VPD, but the younger Robson's route to the police department was by no means predestined.

He'd grown up fast. Summer jobs in construction and commercial fishing during high school left Robson, already just over six feet tall, burly enough to take care of himself in his late teens. At just seventeen he'd worked as an underage bouncer at the Fraser Arms Hotel pub and hung around with members of the Catwalkers motorcycle gang just before it dissolved. He'd even had a run-in with the law when he was arrested for fighting during the 1966 Grey Cup riot. He didn't look much different from many of the East Van ruffians he'd grown up with, so it was no surprise that his first job with the Vancouver Police Department had him playing the part of a would-be culprit.

Al Robson (right) on plainclothes duty in the drug squad. "Nobody ever suspected a guy in an Iron Maiden T-shirt would be a cop."

One night at the Fraser Arms in 1964, Robson met Corporal Paul Campbell of the VPD Canine Unit who was well known across Canada in law enforcement circles as a police dog master. "He knew my father and asked me if I'd like a summer job being a quarryman with the dog squad," Robson says. "A quarryman is the decoy who wears the padded suit and gets chased down by police dogs in training. So I worked running or hiding out at the training field where the dogs would come after me. They were some of the meanest dogs you'd ever seen, I tell you. It was only $3.85 an hour, but I really enjoyed it."

By the time he reached his early twenties, newly married and with a baby, Robson thought that following in his father's footsteps would at least provide a stable income. Yet joining the police department as a young person in the early 1970s in Canada required a confident personality. Considering the volatile political climate of the time, such a career choice could be regarded as a divisive decision among one's peers. Many politically active young people during this era saw police officers as dominating and domineering authority figures. That sentiment became magnified in Vancouver in 1971, the year of the notorious Gastown riot, in which Vancouver police clashed violently with demonstrators who had gathered for a marijuana smoke-in. The VPD was widely criticized for being too heavy-handed with the young demonstrators.

But the politics of the job or how the police were portrayed in the media didn't matter much to Robson, or other new police recruits like him, who disregarded the scorn of friends who accused them of working for "the Man." Some joined because of high ideals—a sense of dedication to public service. Others, like Robson, were simply drawn to the action that such a job promised. In the 1970s, police departments were eager to find young recruits ready to take initiative. People who weren't interested in spending all their time behind a desk. People who were keen to get their hands dirty.

After initially spending his first two years as a patrol officer in South Vancouver's District Three, Robson was seconded to a special duty. "In 1973, I was one of eight guys selected from each district to work a special squad headed by Sergeant Joe Swan," Robson says. After retiring from the police in the 1980s, Swan became a columnist for the *Westender* newspaper, detailing infamous crime stories, and later wrote books about Vancouver police history. "We got nicknamed Swan's Cygnets. I felt fortunate to make the team—and I don't know how I was selected. I was one of the younger guys there, but it was the start of some busy nights in Gastown."

In the early 1970s, Gastown was just beginning to transform from a woebegone semi-industrial area into a new, trendy spot for tourists and locals alike, filled with upmarket restaurants and pubs. Yet many of the shabby old hotel beer parlours along Hastings Street remained and were still pretty rough establishments, places where sex work and drug deals were openly negotiated—in some cases by staff themselves. At the time, narcotics were widely considered one of the main catalysts for urban decay, with police departments across Canada and the US coming down hard on both dealers and users. In this era, police looked just as gravely on possession of marijuana or hash as heroin. Businesses and residences where drug trafficking occurred were often with dealt with more harshly than possession cases involving one individual.

For months in 1973, Vancouver city council had been seeking to cancel the business licences of many Gastown and Downtown Eastside beer parlours, claiming the establishments were poorly run and hosting a staggering amount of illegal activity. The Columbia Hotel pub (303 Columbia Street) had thirty significant police incidents, including a murder, over a four-month period that year, and another nearby bar at the Broadway Hotel (101 East Hastings Street) had more than sixty incidents in the same period. Other infamously shabby beer parlours in the area that saw a lot of police activity were the Balmoral, the New Dodson, and the Anchor Hotel.

Over a two-year period, the Anchor was fined for everything from health to liquor violations. Day and night, drinkers, drug dealers, drug users, sex workers, and even what Robson describes as a group of "Maoist hippies" all held court in the bar. Police doing casual checks in the bar had even had bottles thrown at them, and management did little to discourage this behaviour. Anchor Hotel owner Walter Serrow confessed to the *Province* in 1971: "Sure we have a problem. But it's all over the place ... Suddenly we're in the middle of this political hassle. Sure they [Anchor patrons] are using drugs, but if we try to throw them out, we'd have a riot on our hands."[8] Which is just about what happened one day when Robson and a couple of his fellow special squad members visited the Anchor.

"I went in one afternoon to do a walk-through with a couple of other squad members, Rick Stevens and Ronnie Brown," Robson says. "Stevens had this sixth sense—out of a room full of people he could always tell who the dealers were and who was holding. The bar was full, but he found this gal there with about thirty vials of liquid hash in her purse, selling it out of the place like it was a garage sale on a Sunday afternoon. With that much, we had to take her in. So Rick grabbed her for the arrest, and she started fighting. The next thing you know, the whole place went nuts and turned on us."

What started as pushing and shoving broke into a full-blown melee. Tables were overturned. Beer bottles and smashed glass rained down on the heads of Robson, Stevens, and Brown. With the woman in tow, they retreated to the back wall of the Anchor and into the toilets, radioing for backup. "Ronnie pulled his gun and yelled that the first person who tried to come in would get his brains blown," Robson recalls. "I had my foot up against the door as they were thumping away."

When backup arrived and cleared the bar, the scene settled down. The woman was arrested, along with two Anchor staff members who were also found to be trafficking. But Robson and some squad members returned to the bar at closing time that night. "We took their liquor licence off the wall and shut them down and marched everyone out the door, with about forty arrested for everything from public drunkenness, drug possession, and weapons charges, with a fair number of them who had tried to fight us earlier getting a slap in the face or a

[8] "Police Turn On Heat in Gastown," *Province*, July 24, 1971, 2.

punch in the mouth on the way out," Robson says. He acknowledges that this kind of two-fisted policing was not uncommon in the rougher parts of town.

By 1975, both Gord Bader and Al Robson had been promoted to one of the VPD's crime prevention units (CPUs). Robson and the group he worked with policing Gastown were deemed so successful that they were sent to Granville Street to achieve similar results. The CPUs comprised both uniformed and plainclothes officers and were assigned to focus on certain neighbourhoods, or specific crimes. The posting allowed for more independence, and, most significantly, they were exempt from responding to general police dispatch calls. In a sweeper role over a certain area, CPU officers would only respond if a serious incident was announced on dispatch or if other teams needed additional assistance.

"On the crime prevention units you were sort of left to find your own work," Bader says. He enjoyed the work, initially making two or three arrests a day, but once again felt that his partner wasn't as motivated as he was, and that he could be doing more. It turned out that Robson had similar feelings: "You can be out on the street just biding your time and pick your nose, or you can go out there and go after it and do something."

The two had gotten to know one another after they'd both collared a fellow cop named Stan Atkinson who had been involved in a suspected extortion and debt-collecting operation. Atkinson was discreetly terminated, leading to Robson and Bader's promotion to a CPU. Both men were eager to take on more work. They switched partners and on February 18, 1976, worked their first plainclothes night shift together downtown.[9] "We made six or seven arrests that night, one of a heroin dealer at the Blackstone Hotel on Granville Street," Bader recalls. "It was the start of what felt like a good period, and we started having a lot of nights like that. We were in an unmarked car driving around, but a lot of the time we'd just park it and get on foot and get out there." Both Bader and Robson felt the job had become if not more rewarding, at least more stimulating.

One afternoon Bader and Robson had been surveilling a couple of male suspects, one of whom was believed to be holding a bag containing heroin. When the police officers got out of the car and approached, the man tossed the bag into some nearby bushes. Bader and Robson couldn't tell exactly where it had been thrown and didn't reveal to the detained men that they had even seen the bag. "We said we were police and talked to them for a bit," Bader says, "casually asking if they'd seen somebody we were looking for, and then Al said

[9] Bader kept his police notebooks from those years, which allowed the author to corroborate many dates and details of Bader and Robson's time working together.

he was going to grab a coffee and meet me back at the car." But instead, Robson snuck around behind a corner and hid. "After a couple of minutes I finished talking to them and left and walked back to the car where I could still see them," Bader says. "They stood around for a while and figured after I'd gone nobody was watching them. So the guy reaches back in the bushes and grabs his bag of heroin, thinking he's safe, and just then Al jumped out from behind the corner and yelled, 'Boo!' It was one of the funniest things I'd ever seen. We both sort of felt sorry running the guy in. Al had scared him so bad he'd actually crapped his pants."

It would be one of the many "Al Robson Stories" that circulated the department —stories that garnered him a somewhat infamous reputation among his peers. He was known as the guy who once disarmed a gunman by walking up to him, slapping him across the face, and grabbing the gun out of his hand. He was the guy who observed unconventional parking etiquette: On one occasion, he and another officer had to hurry to catch a flight for an out-of-town conference. Rather than park in the airport's long-term lot, Robson simply left his patrol car parked at the entrance of Vancouver International Airport with a sign on the console reading "On Duty"—an incident that got Robson in hot water with both his superiors and the airport RCMP.

On another occasion, Robson and his colleagues were executing a drug raid at a house, revealing hidden caches of heroin in various rooms. As the occupants of the home sat handcuffed in the living room, a delivery of Chinese food that the dealers had ordered prior to the raid arrived at the door. Rather than turn the delivery person away, Robson paid for it and divided the food among his fellow officers while they continued to catalogue the evidence. The drug dealers looked on in hunger and disbelief.

Younger officers were in awe of Robson's audacity. His contemporaries saw him as either outrageously funny or just plain outrageous. "Al was a nice guy," a fellow Vancouver police officer from Robson's era recalls. "I mean, he'd give you the shirt off his back to help you. But he didn't have a lot of time or patience for some of the politics of the job. I certainly liked him, but I saw how he rubbed some more regimental people the wrong way. You knew he wasn't going to be the kind of guy to ever become chief, but it was pretty clear Al didn't have any interest in that."

Through 1976, Robson and Bader remained on the crime prevention unit, working plainclothes shifts largely focused on Granville Street. South of Nelson

Street in particular, Granville had been plagued by the drug trade since Jeet Pual, one of the biggest street-level dealers in the city, had been shut down. For years, Pual had been trafficking heroin out of his restaurant on the 1100 block of Granville. With Pual sidelined by a 1973 conviction, the trade had splintered and spread. Using restaurants as drug trafficking fronts was not uncommon downtown. The Chick and Bull at 1202 Granville and the Plaza Cafe at 100 East Hastings had both been used for trafficking not only by dealers who dined there but also by restaurant staff. Meanwhile, at the Blue Eagle Cafe at 130 East Hastings, the heroin problem among its patrons was so rampant that the owner drilled holes in the spoons so customers wouldn't steal them to use for shooting up.

After the Penthouse Nightclub was shut down, and sex workers spread out into other areas of the downtown core, Bader and Robson continued to get plenty of work to fill their shift. In particular, they regularly assisted vice squad units deployed downtown, as well as with other various incidents that occurred in the area.

"There was always a roundup that happened once a year," Bader recalls. "They'd gather the troops at Main Street of just about everybody who was on shift over the course of a few days, pass out photos of everyone who had outstanding warrants out for their arrest, and really just cut us loose all over the city. It was almost a way to see who could make the most arrests. But within that first hour, the people we were looking for made themselves scarce as word got out there was a roundup going on. So it got harder to find people over the course of the next couple of days. You might get one or two more, but people went underground."

In the wake of a roundup, with some time on their hands, Bader and Robson read reports coming from the Hudson's Bay department store building at Granville and Georgia and complaints filed to police of men having sex in the toilet stalls of the fourth-floor restroom. "Initially, there were just reports from customers coming in to use the washroom, and overhearing the noise, seeing two men in a single stall. So we went down to see what was happening, and I tell you we were pretty shocked it was so rampant and frequent," Bader recalls. "The store security supervisor was this short Irishman who referred to the 'jam tarts'—as he called them—using the place. They were apparently keeping an eye on it, but they weren't doing a very good job it seemed."

These weren't the type of suspects who dodged court appearances or the repeat offenders targeted in the annual roundup, but with little else to do at the moment, Bader and Robson went to investigate. Conducting some rudimentary stakeouts that even Hudson's Bay staff were unaware of, Bader and Robson posed in plain clothes as shoppers and observed the washroom entrance from behind the clothing aisles. If one man walked in not long after another, either Bader or Robson would wait a minute and walk in to check, appearing as if they needed to use the facilities. If they found the men were using separate stalls and obviously not together, there was no issue. But if they overheard an unmistakable grunting and saw two pairs of legs in one stall, they would detain the individuals and escort them to an office. Police tried to keep the arrests discreet. If shoppers noticed the men being taken away, they might have thought it was for shoplifting and not gross indecency, a charge that was used to prosecute gay men engaged in sexual activity and was removed from Canada's Criminal Code in 1985.

"It was a pretty wide array of people from all walks of life involved," Bader says. "Guys from their early twenties to middle age. We ended up arresting everyone from priests to a US border patrol officer. We ended up even catching the Irishman who was the store security. The whole thing was pretty eye-opening."

"I couldn't personally care less what one person wants to stick into somebody else, as long as it's not a knife," Robson says brusquely. "Go ahead, do what you want to do, as long as you're not killing anybody—or yourself. Today maybe it would be overlooked, or just handled differently. But you have to understand, in 1976, politely standing on the toilet, looking over the stalls, shooing fellas away and telling them to please move along wasn't done. It was happening in such a public place and just had been reported so often we couldn't ignore it."

As surprised as Bader and Robson might have been by the situation, the Hudson's Bay washroom had been used as a space for discreet encounters for months, perhaps even years. The fourth-floor men's room could be considered part of the early history of secret gay meeting places in the city, particularly before gay liberation ushered in openly queer nightclubs. Around the same time, there were reports of a similar situation occurring at the English Bay bathhouse public washroom. Bader and Robson were asked to go to Davie and Denman to investigate. Colleagues teased the pair about their new position as the VPD's public-toilet crime experts. The detail didn't exactly provide the dignity or status that Bader had been looking for. Robson tried to make the best of it by joking sardonically that their career had "gone down the toilet." But when they found out the true nature of the complaints, it stopped being a joking matter.

Since the early 1900s, when legendary local lifeguard Joe Fortes taught children to swim in the ocean, English Bay had been a popular recreational destination in the West End. Built in 1931, the bathhouse contained both a change room and public washrooms for the hundreds of swimmers who came to the beach daily. The concrete structure is still there, just east of the Cactus Club restaurant, but by the late 1970s, the building had deteriorated—both structurally and in terms of what went on inside. "There were mothers who had sent their boys into the men's washrooms, and some of the kids were being assaulted or groped," Robson recalls gravely. Adults having consensual encounters in a department store washroom was one thing—but now kids were involved.

The bathhouse wasn't as easy to monitor as the Hudson's Bay men's room. At the beach, police would often be forced to stake out inside the bathroom itself, in a stall where they would wait for two men to enter another stall. Occasionally, once caught, occupants would refuse to come out, and Robson says he was not above throwing a cup of water over the stall to roust them. Suspects would also sometimes bolt from the stalls, and Bader and Robson would often decide not to chase, hoping they'd made their point.

The officers were once shocked to discover a thirteen-year-old boy in the stalls who had been meeting men there. "We didn't arrest him, but we figured his parents were concerned he was acting out that way at that age. They had no idea what was going on until we brought him home. He'd been skipping school in the afternoon to go down there. He did end up telling us about a bunch of other places in the city like at the Woodward's department store and even up at the Langara campus building where the same sort of activity was occurring."

Most of those found using the bathhouse washroom weren't sex workers, though some were. Robson argues against the suggestion that police were targeting the gay community with these kinds of stakeouts. He says it was no different from answering a noise complaint for a party that had gotten out of hand. "There were a lot of complaints—from hotels and cafés from one end of the beach to the other, from the Sylvia Hotel up to the bathhouse area on Denman Street—that people out for an evening stroll were bumping into people having sex or being propositioned themselves. They had every right to walk through there without that happening, so at that point it couldn't just be ignored."

Since the late 1960s, English Bay had developed a reputation as a nocturnal cruising area for men, in particular around some of the logs on the beach. To everyday beachgoers, the logs on the beach provided an area to sit on or stretch

The English Bay bathhouse today.

out by, but at night they found a different purpose. The logs were numbered on each end, and these numbers were used to specify particular meeting spots. "We used to call Sunset Beach 'Bitch Beach,'" laughs seventy-three-year-old Art Robinson, who grew up in the Vancouver suburb of Coquitlam. Aware at a young age that he was gay, Robinson moved to the West End when he was twenty. "The cruising scene around the beach really wasn't my thing, but everybody knew it was the case."

Word also got around that the police were monitoring the bathhouse, leaving only those who were unaware of the clampdown and those more blatantly soliciting sex work to get caught. Outside of catching someone in the act, the chances of a successful arrest and charge were negligible. "It was always a bit of a sorry sight when we arrested some married man for gross indecency or picking up a hustler, and his wife had to come down and pick him up," Robson says. "She'd be down at the police station in tears, seated with all sorts of other people whose husbands or sons were in for worse, so we tried when we could to seat them elsewhere, away from the others." Robson grimly recalls that stakeouts like these at the bathhouse were suddenly and quietly discontinued by VPD supervisors. The officers were discreetly informed later that this was because police had learned an alarming number of married men who had been arrested in these situations had committed suicide.

But even if activity at the public washroom was temporarily halted, the immediate area was still used for cruising and sex work. In the aftermath, the city decided to refrain from involving the heavier hand of law enforcement and settled on measures that probably would have been more suitable to begin with. The city put in more street lights to brighten the area at night and installed new washroom stall doors that only went as high as just over waist level with the aim of limiting privacy to discourage sexual encounters.

And so it came to be that on this English Bay detail Bader and Robson found themselves in an unmarked police car parked off Davie and Denman Street, surveilling the comings and goings around the bathhouse in September 1976. The radio played songs like Gordon Lightfoot's "The Wreck of the Edmund Fitzgerald," Blue Öyster Cult's "(Don't Fear) The Reaper," and the tune that played everywhere that summer, ABBA's "Dancing Queen."

Bader and Robson could not have imagined what was in store for them. At the time, neither considered the posting in English Bay to be especially prestigious. Even their colleagues in the vice squad—which was not a duty every police officer relished—seemed to be dealing with juicier police work. The two chose to simply treat it as any other kind of call that might last several days, and then turn back to other work like the drug arrests they'd done within the crime prevention unit.

During this period, the officers noticed a number of teenage boys who, both alone and in small groups, wandered the area along Davie Street to English Bay. They didn't appear to be neighbourhood schoolkids skipping class or West End latchkey kids out late at night. These were young hustlers.

Bader and Robson began walking the beat and, through casual conversation, eventually earned the trust of some of the hustlers. What had started as an assignment to follow up on some neighbourhood complaints that yielded a handful of gross indecency arrests quickly developed into something much bigger. The police officers learned that most of the hustlers were runaways from different parts of the city, some even from other parts of the province. Many of them were pushouts—children whose parents had evicted them, didn't wish to hear from them again, and did not report them missing. Almost all of them had come here because even the instability of life on the streets was preferable to their abusive home lives. Most came from low-income households and had grim personal histories of physical or sexual abuse. If they were charged here with vagrancy, they would only be sent back to those same homes, and they'd soon be back on the streets of the West End again in an increasingly desperate cycle of neglect. Many had been drawn to hustling as an easy way to make money—easier than mugging, robbing, or pushing drugs. And the boys were seldom charged with soliciting, so it was easier to avoid prosecution. But this lifestyle was not without its hazards. Even after just a few months on the street, the stress and psychological trauma would age many well beyond their years.

One West End hustler Bader and Robson got to know was named Mark. At just seventeen, Mark said he had been hustling for five years. In that time, he'd moved around between Seattle and Portland, then to Edmonton, but here in Vancouver he had gained regular customers—many of them married men.

"I'm choosy. I pick the guys I go with," Mark told the officers. He said he made fifty or sixty dollars a night, though he thought he could make more if he hustled harder. He lived in a West End apartment with a group of boys that had essentially become his family. "My parents are around somewhere, but I don't want anything to do with them."[10]

Mark's life on the street was supported by the indestructible confidence that one might expect from a seventeen-year-old boy with precocious street smarts. He was buoyant and gregarious, with an air of authority. Mark seemed to know everyone in Vancouver's gay scene, young and old, as well as every bartender

[10] Mark's words are taken from a later *Province* interview.

and restaurant proprietor in the West End. He lived in a way that most would consider reckless, or at least aimless—spending his money as quickly as he made it, usually blowing half a night's earnings on drinks, meeting his friends who lived as he did in clubs and diners, where they could gossip, laugh, and smoke too much.

Mark talked a lot. Bader and Robson got to know him quickly. Basic conversations with him often led to darker, more grim details about Mark's lifestyle as he let his guard down. He confessed to participating in pornographic films and photo shoots. He revealed that the same man who had organized these sessions had once also directed him and others to blackmail or steal from some clients—along with teaching them advanced tricks of the hustler's trade. He told them that being in a john's car after sex provided an opportunity to steal his wallet and learn his identity. A hustler could then demand money and threaten to reveal the john's sexual preferences to his family. The john would be too embarrassed, the man reasoned, to go to the police.

The man paid the boys with the promise of drink, drugs, or a place to stay. When the bill added up the man pushed them to prostitution—a term that was never used. It was just a matter of "I helped you, and now you need to help me." This was how these vulnerable teenagers were introduced to wealthy men in the West End who paid for sex with underage boys.

Bader and Robson were unsure what to do with this information at first. But the man in question came up again in conversations with other boys like Mark.

"That's where we first heard the name Wayne Harris," Bader says.

CHAPTER 5

Bars and Bathhouses

"I remember when Wayne Harris first showed up in Vancouver," recalls seventy-four-year-old Dennis Robbins, who became the manager of Faces nightclub in 1970—the same year that Wayne Harris arrived in Vancouver from Halifax. "He was friendly and good-looking, about five foot ten and well built, with sandy blond hair. We got along well. Wayne was talkative and wasn't shy. I wasn't scared of him, but I certainly knew other people were. And there were reasons for that."

Robbins had arrived in Vancouver from Ontario in 1968 at the age of twenty-one at a time when a lot of young gay men from across Canada, like him and Harris, were drawn to the West Coast with its promise of fine summers, mild winters, and the city's growing reputation of being the "San Francisco of Canada," with the West End considered to be its epicentre as *the* gay-friendly neighbourhood.

As soon as Robbins arrived in town, he headed for English Bay. On his way past a construction site at the foot of the Burrard Street Bridge, he was stopped by police who asked him what he was up to. "I told them I was headed to the beach to see the Pacific Ocean," Robbins says.

"Don't you know that homosexuals walk up and down there all night long?" the police asked.

"No, I didn't know that," Robbins replied. The police left him, and he rushed to the beach.

It was the start of a new life for him at the dawn of a period of gay liberation in Vancouver. Within two months he was living in a West End penthouse, and a year later, he was managing Faces—the most popular gay club in town.

It began as a club called Twiggy's in 1968, changed its name a year later to the 795 Club (after its address at 795 Seymour Street), and finally became Faces in 1970, which it remained for years. Faces was located at the corner of Robson and Seymour, on the ground floor of the Orillia, a mixed-use structure built in 1903. Gone, and nearly forgotten, today, Faces was known for playing progressive

Photo by Lloyd Nicholson

Outside of Faces nightclub at 795 Seymour Street, just prior to its demolition in 1985. The space was a popular gay nightspot through the 1970s and early '80s. Note the U-Frame-It outlet across the street (at left); more on U-Frame-It in Chapter 6.

music and for being an early LGBTQ-friendly establishment. "It was the first gay club I ever went to when I got to town. I'd never been in one before. I went in all by myself—I was actually scared!" Robbins laughs. "But I liked it."

Without a liquor licence, Faces operated as a private club where patrons had to buy an annual membership (for one dollar) and sign in upon entry. Members could also bring their own bottles of alcohol as long as they were checked in at the bar. Faces played Motown music when it first opened but later featured early disco, which at the time was scarcely heard at any of the mainstream clubs in town. In the years before the local alternative club scene flourished at Luv-a-Fair, Faces was *the* place to go if you wanted to hear some of the city's early DJs spin music from the US and Europe.

The very nature of Faces clientele unintentionally added a certain mystique to the place. "Unlike in the straight clubs, many of our patrons were afraid to use their own names, which is probably how Marlene Dietrich, Joan Crawford, and

Mae West became Faces members," Robbins noted in a piece he wrote for *Xtra! West* newspaper in 2006.[11] Today, he recalls, "It was a pretty hip crowd who went there and a wide mix of ages. Even Robert Plant and Jimmy Page came in one night after Led Zeppelin played in town, and Lou Reed came once, too."

Of the thousands who passed through the club's doors over its few years, one person who stands out in Robbins's memory is Wayne Harris.

"I liked Wayne," Robbins says. "But within a couple of years of him getting into town, he fell in as the leader of a ring of Granville Street hustlers who were real thugs. One Saturday night they came into Faces—it was a busy night and the music was up. Wayne started causing a bit of a scene—being disruptive, rowdy—that was bothering other people. I realized I had to step in, so I went over to talk to ask him and his friends to leave. But he grabbed me, threw me to the floor, jumped on top of me, and put a knife to my throat."

Wayne Harris arrived in Vancouver in the early 1970s and lived above the Taurus bathhouse. By the end of the decade he would be the central focus of a major vice squad investigation.

Author archives

Someone cut the music, the lights were turned up, and silence rapidly spread across the room. There was no bouncer at Faces to assist; there had never been a need for one. Whether out of shock, uncertainty, or fear of Harris, everybody held back from getting involved.

"I just tried to keep my cool, to keep him calm," Robbins remembers. "Telling him, 'I thought we were friends,' saying he couldn't do this sort of thing in the place. I did most of the talking. I didn't feel necessarily in danger, because it felt like he was doing the whole thing for show—for his friends, showing he was a tough guy. I think he was aware that somebody had called the police. And I just told him if he ever wanted to come in here again, he had to leave."

After a few moments, Harris jumped up—said nothing—and stormed out with his entourage.

[11] Dennis Robbins, "The Faces of Our Youth," *Xtra! West*, December 6, 2006.

It was either a busy night for the police or an incident that was deemed low priority, because they arrived late—nearly twenty minutes after the initial call. Robbins outlined the events for the police, even named Harris specifically, but was left confused by their response. The patrol officers told Robbins that the gay bars were largely "left alone" by police. Robbins felt he could take this one of two ways: the officers were suggesting that they wanted to leave clubs like Faces free from harassment, such as unnecessarily checking patrons' identification—or, more bluntly, the officers were saying, *You're on your own.*

The relationship between police and the gay community in Vancouver had reached its nadir in the 1970s. Police were arresting men in gay cruising areas, and although they rarely did so in gay-friendly bars, they were not above it. In the early '70s, police would occasionally shine flashlights in patrons' faces during bar walk-throughs and take names, threatening to publish them. In June 1973, police entered the Hampton Court Club, a gay nightclub at 1066 Seymour Street, and photographed everyone inside. The Hampton closed shortly afterward. There would be a number of raids in gay after-hours clubs and bathhouses the following year, most of which went unreported by the local television news and print media.

These were the early days of openly gay bars operating in Vancouver. While many in the LGBTQ community lived near Davie Street and frequented restaurants along that strip, if an occasion called for drinking, dancing, and socializing, they often headed east of Granville to the many gay bars along Seymour Street.

From Champagne Charlie's at the corner of Seymour and Davie (612 Davie Street) to the Playpen Central (856 Seymour Street) and the hotel bars at the Dufferin (900 Seymour Street), a remarkable number of gay bars and LGBTQ-friendly establishments sprang up in Vancouver in the 1970s—all of which were within walking distance from the West End. Some places were more discreet than others, but even if these were still the outwardly cautious, early days of gay nightclubs in Vancouver, that didn't mean the action inside was reserved. "It was a joyous and carefree time in Vancouver back then," says sixty-four-year-old George Pruden, who first started going to Faces at fifteen. "There was a strong, gay-driven art scene back then," he recalls. "We referred to each other as the 'friends of Dorothy,' after Judy Garland in *The Wizard of Oz*. We were cuter, wittier, and dressed better than the straight boys!"

Those nights the bars were full of "Castro Street clones," a nickname referring to the gay district in San Francisco. This meant young men dressed very similarly, as though in uniform: tight shirts, Frye boots, and Levi's 501 jeans. Marijuana was ubiquitous. Cocaine had yet to come into prominent use—the nightlife was frenetic enough, as nightspots often changed names and themes overnight. The Bullring (887 Seymour Street) later became the Corral Club and eventually the Dance Machine. Other places had more unassuming, anonymous monikers, like the 616 Club, named for its address at 616 Robson Street.

With their high-quality light and sound systems, Faces and the Gandydancer (1222 Hamilton Street) became popular with the dance crowds. But many clubs were smoky, dark spaces that could hardly be considered upscale. Previously known as the August Club, the Shaggy Horse (818 Richards

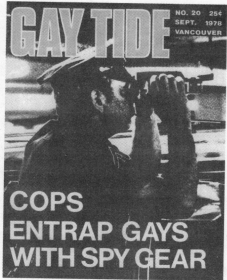

c/o Don Hann

The relationship between the police and the gay community was at its nadir in the 1970s, with complaints that the police were targeting gay nightspots and cruising areas.

Street) had shag carpeting on the walls that over time became alarmingly grimy with the stains of cigarette smoke and spilled beer, and washrooms that had waist-level mirrors next to the urinals that allowed a patron to easily get a peek at his neighbour. Perhaps the most notorious venue was the after-hours Playpen South (1369 Richards Street), one of three Playpen clubs that became home to Vancouver's leather scene and reeked of amyl nitrate, or poppers. These narcotics brought a rush of dizziness and euphoria, relaxing both inhibitions and muscles to facilitate the sex that took place in the recesses of the club.

There was also a variety of lesbian clubs operating in Vancouver during the 1970s. The bar of the Vanport Hotel (635 Main Street) was a well-known meeting place, as was Queenie's Truck Stop (1135 Howe Street), in the back of Club Zanzibar. Before it turned into the rock 'n' roll bar Club Soda, and later the Starfish Room, the Quadra Club (1055 Homer Street) began as lesbian bar that was also open to gay men, just as Faces welcomed women. For the day drinkers, the Ambassador Hotel bar opened every morning—"Where the beer was cheap and the clientele was cheaper," jokes Pruden.

One thing all these gay clubs had in common: they offered safe refuge at night. Many gay clubgoers of the era recall walking home and having slurs barked and hissed at them from passing cars. The anxiety this caused in gay men went hand in hand with their fear that they could just as easily become the victim of gay bashing.

Although the gay clubs did offer refuge from this kind of abuse, Pruden believes that the never-ending celebration of frivolity and liberation inside those clubs bred its own kind of trouble. "There was also a kind of predatory environment then," he says. "I was young. I rarely paid for my drinks. I guess I was naive back then. I just thought they were interesting gay older men."

There were plenty who were just that—those who simply enjoyed some youthful company, someone to chat with at the bar or even to dance with. There were also those who acted as platonic mentors for young gay men. But there were others, who drifted through the nightclub culture of drink and drugs, who seemed to be on the lookout for especially young boys or men to prey upon. There was even a slang term for these older men—chicken hawks.

Wayne Harris was only twenty-three when he arrived in Vancouver in 1970—too young, perhaps, to be a chicken hawk, but he certainly had accrued the experience of an older man. He had been a hustler since the age of twelve, after a childhood spent in twenty-two different foster homes. He'd come to Vancouver for the reason so many others did: the promise of a fresh start in a city—new people, new opportunities, and new schemes. Harris came with an agenda and personality that he'd developed and honed over years on the streets. Many of a certain age in the West End's gay community remember his good traits. He could be generous, friendly, and quick-witted—enjoyable company. His charisma and good looks could easily charm and disarm those who couldn't see that he was sizing them up. But the years of being used by others when he was younger had taught him that, no matter what, he needed to look out for himself above all. Many were intimidated by him. Decades after Harris arrived in Vancouver, many gay residents who were living in the city at the time and were interviewed for this book still remember him. Many recall being so intimidated by him that Harris seems like a figure that his own nightmares would be afraid of. Yet others remember him as likeable and friendly, and he used his charm to befriend hustlers, or win the trust of young runaways new to the streets and manipulate them. He had the perfect skill set and personality to become a pimp—which is exactly what he did.

The Rialto Hotel at 1140 Granville Street, early 1970s.

Harris arrived in Vancouver with his boyfriend and right-hand man, Ray Paris. Less is known about Paris's life story, except that he was Black and slightly taller than Harris. Paris didn't have Harris's garrulous charm and charisma, but he did have the same ability to intimidate.

"I had no use for pimps. I didn't like them," says seventy-three-year-old Art Robinson, recalling Harris. Robinson worked at the 795 Club and later at Faces as a greeter. He bused tables and oversaw the music playlist at the club. "I was one of those ditzy-type people you'd see in clubs," he laughs. "When I was twenty, I looked sixteen!"

"There were some tough characters around back then in Vancouver in the early 1970s," Robinson remembers. "I've never really discussed with other people my feelings about them until now. But people like Harris and Paris really instilled fear into people, and that sticks in my mind. They were bullies. Paris was a real sleazebag."

Robinson recalls that it was well known that Harris had taken over the upstairs of the Rialto Hotel at 1140 Granville Street, filling the upstairs room with young boys working for him as a stable of hustlers. "He didn't have just one or two boys but a flock of them," Robinson says. "At least half a dozen. I tried to warn people not to have anything to do with him, even just being social. But some just got drawn in."

Built in 1912, the Rialto Hotel had seen better days by the 1930s, located above the Peter Pan Café that was run by Peter Pantages and his brothers, one of Vancouver's most prominent families in the entertainment industry. But by the 1950s, it had acquired the reputation of a flophouse, and by the 1970s, as the crime rate on Granville Street rose, the hotel became a regular venue for police arrests for everything from drunken assaults to heroin trafficking. Rumours circulated that, beyond the sex trade he oversaw, Harris was using the rooms to produce pornography and traffic drugs. Either with threats, blandishments, or bribes, he managed to avoid interference from the hotel clerks.

It's difficult to ascertain when exactly Harris launched his operation in the Rialto rooms. It seems to have gone unnoticed for a while by Vancouver law enforcement. But while Harris may have had a knack for evading police, one of his associates almost caught up with him in July 1975. One night, Harris was standing at the corner of Seymour and Helmcken Streets when he was shot at by an assailant with a shotgun, causing Harris to dive for cover behind a parked car. The shooter, forty-two-year-old Robert Bellyea, was arrested, though his motive was unclear, and court records of this incident have long since been expunged. Regardless, it was clear that Harris had enemies.

Harris lived for a period in the Bon Accord Hotel at 1233 Hornby Street, above the notorious Taurus bathhouse. Opened in the 1930s, the Bon Accord had a full steam-bath facility that became a popular amenity for many West End residents whose accommodations didn't have sufficient bathing facilities. By the 1970s, the hotel had become more of a rundown rooming house. The bathhouse, meanwhile, became popular among many gay West Enders and developed a reputation for promiscuity. The Taurus would eventually be shut down for the sex work that occurred within its walls. Operators of the bathhouse were charged with keeping a common bawdy house, as well as contributing to juvenile delinquency. It was rebranded the El Toro under new management, but the 1970s were the years when the establishment partied with unbridled abandon.

"The rooms were typical of a rooming house, with a bunk bed on top," says former resident Andre Tardif. "Jamie Lee Hamilton worked the front door, where you could get towels and buy food—just little microwaveable things and whatnot. Later, I moved down the hall because it overlooked a big space downstairs—a room with a view. There would always be some hanky-panky going on downstairs, and I could always go down and check out the buffet."

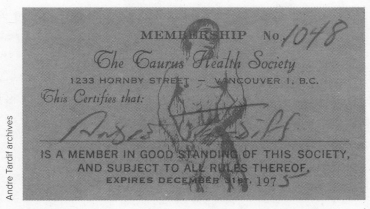

Andre Tardif's membership card to the Taurus bathhouse.

Now sixty-eight years old, Tardif has a bright, upbeat demeanour and fondly recalls Vancouver in the 1970s. Born and raised in Quebec, he retains a light French Canadian accent. Prior to coming to Vancouver, he worked as a twenty-one-year-old hustler in Toronto near the St. Charles Tavern, a noted gay meeting place. "I didn't do well. I always looked older. So I was the last to get picked up! I didn't look like a twink," he says.

Tardif had always thought of coming to Vancouver and in September 1974 hitchhiked with two friends, also French Canadian hustlers, and went straight to the Taurus. "There were rooms upstairs there you could rent for twelve hours, or by the week for just twenty-two dollars." Tardif embraced the freewheeling lifestyle at the Bon Accord, so much so that within two months he'd contracted syphilis. "The Taurus was crawling with hustlers, and I suppose at that time I fit right in," Tardif says. "I ended up getting treated at Vancouver General Hospital but eventually moved out of the Taurus within a couple of months after that."

Vancouver's bathhouses had been a target of the morality squad going back to the 1940s. In 1965, Vancouver's chief medical officer Dr Joseph Gayton suggested that some bathhouses were responsible for an increase in cases of venereal disease and urged regulations be put in place to ensure that bathhouse cubicles be adequately lit and have their doors removed to reduce privacy. Police and public concern over the bathhouses would only grow in subsequent years.

"There were a lot of people connecting at the Taurus for free," Tardif remembers. "But other people were paying. Twenty dollars was the average." In September 1975, a report prepared for the BC Police Commission by Monique Layton, a graduate student at the University of British Columbia, noted that there were more than 700 sex workers working in downtown Vancouver, with an estimated total annual income of more than $30 million. Of these, there were between 100 and 150 regular male hustlers ranging in age from twelve to twenty-five, with the majority between fifteen and nineteen. Although Tardif recalls young hustlers at the Taurus bathhouse at that time, he doesn't remember any as young as twelve. He acknowledges, however, that this could have started happening by the beginning of 1975, after he'd moved out of the Bon Accord Hotel.

Aside from the concerns expressed by city health officials and the occasional mention in city council meetings of shutting down the bathhouses altogether, the issue never garnered enough interest to effect change. A VPD drug squad investigation in the mid-1970s spurred by an informant who reported drug deals occurring in the bathhouses never amounted to much. But bathhouse visits were often memorable for officers. Al Robson recalls an incident from early in his police career. "[Constable] Ronnie Brown and I went in [the Taurus] one night when we were in uniform," Robson says. "There was a warrant for a guy who was suspected to be in there. I honestly don't think police had ever really ever been in the place. So we walked right into the main room and shone our flashlights around and turned the lights on. There must have been twenty naked guys oiled up all over one another. They scattered like hell when they saw us. I just burst out laughing and walked out shaking my head—there was a better time to do this, for everybody. Later, one of the sergeants asked us if we'd picked up the suspect there, and I said, 'You try and find one guy amongst a pile of twenty greased-up fellas all running away. It would have been like pig wrestling in a muddy barnyard.'"

Sometime in 1975, Wayne Harris's hustlers were turfed out of the Rialto, and Harris moved to Surrey to lie low, before he eventually moved back into town, just outside the West End and over the Burrard Street Bridge to the Kitsilano neighbourhood.

"Harris was well connected, and he had quite an operation," Gord Bader recalls. By the time he came to the attention of Bader and Robson in 1975, Harris had an arrest record going back to 1970, the year he'd arrived in Vancouver. The list of charges covered everything from narcotics possession to possession of a prohibited weapon to making threats. Somehow, he had managed to either avoid conviction or get off with a fine or a few days in jail. But it was the rumours that police heard about Harris pimping underage boys to older men in the West End that triggered a wider, more rigorous investigation into his activities.

Bader and Robson's reports on Harris eventually reached Detective Jim Maitland. Born in Scotland, Maitland had joined the VPD in 1962, at the age of twenty-three, and had worked his way up from patrol and combined law enforcement unit investigations to make detective with the vice squad in 1976. He'd worked in the VPD's notorious H-Squad, its gang task force, that had been tasked four years earlier with going after the Clark Park Gang in the aftermath of a violent incident outside a Rolling Stones concert at the Pacific Coliseum in East Vancouver. Over the course of a thirty-five-year career, with occasional seconding and transfers, Maitland spent fourteen years on the VPD vice squad, which included half a dozen of the VPD's grimmest child exploitation and human trafficking investigations.

"As a detective, I probably spent more time in vice than just about anybody else through that time," says eighty-two-year-old Maitland, in a light Scottish brogue, even though he has lived in Canada for decades. He looks back fondly on his police career, despite the many dark investigations he carried out. He also witnessed Vancouver undergo a significant transformation over those years on the job. "The West End changed a lot in my time there," he says. "In the beginning, when I was working as a beat officer, it was actually very seldom you'd see a gay couple. We had some domestic squabbles—some fights between gay couples—but that's about it. But by the 1970s, the problems with street prostitution were rampant, and West End crime had really grown. There were major crimes and kidnappings we were dealing with that never really became public."

The vice squad was kept busy dealing with sex work on Georgia and Granville Streets, as well increasingly on Davie Street, but initially male sex workers were not deemed a priority. There appeared to be fewer of them, and they tended to roam, not yet working from a specific location. But Bader and Robson's street-level investigation triggered a closer look at Harris at the same time that others on the vice squad were beginning to hear his name in connection with young men arrested for sex work. Harris and Paris gradually become better known to the police. Although they had apparently ended their romantic relationship, they remained business partners in their criminal enterprise. Only now there was a third person involved: twenty-two-year-old Helga Harris, who was Wayne's common-law wife.

Helga had come to Vancouver from Manitoba and had developed an addiction to heroin. She was doing sex work on Davie Street to support her habit, using the street name Joanne when she first met Wayne. Injection tracks on her arm showed that the drugs had begun to take their toll, but her relationship with Harris presented an even greater threat to her well-being.

"Harris became Helga's pimp, and Paris was her lookout while she was working," Maitland recalls. "Ray Paris would also steer young juvenile males to Wayne. They were quite a group. But what we discovered beyond that was they operated as a modern-day Fagin enterprise. Once Wayne had established a familiarity with the boys, he was having them commit B and Es [breaking and entering] on residences near the Harris home."

Harris knew what would sell, or what he could easily fence. Cash and jewellery were always the best items to find hidden in a home. TV sets in the 1970s were as heavy as large pieces of furniture, so it often required a car to move a stolen TV from a home, but radios and expensive clothing like furs could be easily bundled and stolen. But "the burglaries and stolen goods were only a small part of our interest," Maitland says. Police had also discovered that Harris was providing his best thieves with alcohol, drugs, and sex with either Helga or himself.

"Our greater concern," Maitland emphasizes, "became the pedophile aspect." Reports had led officers to suspect that Harris was trafficking many of the underage street kids he had under his influence to wealthy male clients—police just didn't know the names of who was involved.

"That's when we started the wiretap."

CHAPTER 6

Dirty Books and Dirty Looks

Vancouver police were committed to disabling the Wayne Harris crime ring. But their efforts were temporarily diverted by the actions of newly elected Vancouver mayor Jack Volrich, who had taken office at the beginning of 1977 and decided that the most immediate crime threat to Vancouver was pornography.

Today, of course, pornography is easily accessed for free with the cost of an internet connection. In 1977, before the ubiquity of home computers, before X-rated videotapes could easily be rented and viewed at home on a VCR, acquiring pornography required a more effort, usually via a discreet trip to an adult book and magazine store or sex shop.

Jack Volrich's call to arms was not the first time the Vancouver vice squad dealt with a case of obscene material—at least in books and magazines. In September 1964, vice had raided the Fraser Book Bin at 1247 Granville Street, charging store owner Ted Fraser and three of his employees with possession of obscene matter for the purpose of distribution. Offending titles ranged from *Whip Me: Some More My Lady, Pals of Pain, Court of Spanking Relations,* and *Sinning Teacher,* along with copies of *The Catcher in the Rye.* And it wasn't just pulp magazine stores that were targeted. A year later, Bill Duthie of venerable Vancouver institution Duthie Books was raided over stocking Hubert Selby Jr.'s infamously candid novel *Last Exit to Brooklyn,* which had been ruled obscene. Losing court battles locally prompted both Duthie and Fraser to fight their cases all the way to the Supreme Court of Canada, where they also lost. Eventually, in 1968, in a landmark censorship case in the UK, the book was dropped from most obscenity lists.

On the first day of spring in March 1977, Volrich led a team of licence inspectors on visits to five downtown book and magazine shops along the 1000 block of Granville Street, which was a perfect battleground for the moral fight that played out. Although Granville Street north of Nelson—with its theatre row, including the Orpheum and the Vogue, as well as several cinemas—still held some prestige, the Granville Strip south of Nelson was dotted with down-at-the-heels diners, old beer parlours, pawnshops, and used book and magazine stores.

Volrich sought to ban a variety of adult publications, including mass-market magazines such as *Playboy* and *Penthouse,* but his immediate target was magazines that featured photos of naked children. Volrich stated that these publications could "only be designed for people who may have perverse habits." But Volrich didn't just want them off Vancouver magazine shelves; he also wanted to go after the source.

One of the magazines seized, *Nudist Moppets,* was published in California by a company run by Reuben Sturman, a Cleveland-based mobster with connections to the Gambino crime family in New York. Sturman had started a magazine distribution company in the 1960s that became the biggest distributor of adult magazines across America and had even been credited with the invention of the peep show booth. He was later dubbed the "Walt Disney of Porn" for his monopolizing, corporatizing effect on the pornography industry.

Almost none of the pornography that the vice squad seized in Vancouver was produced locally. The magazines had come through Sturman's distribution company and were imported into Canada by Tony Perry, whose Fantasy Factory adult video stores still have outlets in the Lower Mainland today. When questioned, Perry said the magazines had been approved by Canada Customs. He volunteered that "if somebody in authority at the local level has any objections, they should just let us know and we'll withdraw it. I'm just trying to make a living, not break the law."[12]

Perry's brother Peter was involved in organized crime in Montreal, and for years both police and the media speculated that, with his connections to Sturman's companies, Tony was also involved in organized crime. Perry even had some of Sturman's peep show booths in his Vancouver retail stores. But Perry was confirmed to have no Mafia connections and was merely an entrepreneur whose recession-proof business selling magazines and sex toys (then often marketed as "marital aids") had made him wealthy. Perry was smart enough to keep his warehouse in the suburb of Burnaby, just beyond the city limits and outside the jurisdiction for raids by Vancouver police.

There might have been more to Volrich's anti-pornography campaign than his personal disdain for the material. The bookstore raids were deliberately synchronized with the opening of the new Chateau Granville Hotel. Volrich's busts also coincided with more police presence and clampdowns on sex work

[12] "Isobutyl Nitrite Is Prohibited," *Vancouver Sun*, January 6, 2001, A13.

along Granville Street. Skeptics believed that gentrification, rather than moral rectitude, had been on the mayor's mind. Volrich himself stated later that August that he hoped increased police presence would encourage more "desirable development," like the new hotel.

In the end, it was left to the Vancouver police vice squad to throw cold water on Volrich's anti-pornography crusade. Staff Sergeant Glenn McDonald, the new head of the squad, had to inform Volrich that the federal government had approved the importation of precisely the kind of pornographic books and magazines that the mayor wanted banned. McDonald wasn't pleased with this development either. "If there's one thing I hated, it was pornography," the eighty-five-year-old MacDonald says today. "I constantly had to see or read the stuff that was current, to be informed about it, and the worst stuff was pretty sickening."

Staff Sgt. Glenn McDonald became the new head of the VPD vice squad in 1975.

McDonald had witnessed a lot over his career on the streets—not just vulgarity and decadence but also violence and death. Yet he has a surprisingly charming and jovial manner. A 1977 article in the *Province* newspaper pegged him as a dead ringer for the actor Gary Cooper. ("Boy, I took a lot of ribbing from the other guys for that," MacDonald recalls.) He still possesses a rich baritone voice that might have helped him become a dramatic actor if he'd decided on a different career. But he admits that ever since he was about five years old, he'd dreamed about becoming a police officer.

Those dreams were probably inspired by McDonald's father, who had joined the VPD in 1929, and then returned to the force after the Second World War as a vice squad detective, though McDonald doesn't recall his father talking much about the job, or the war. "A lot of those guys were the strong and silent type, and had PTSD—but they didn't know what it was called back then," says MacDonald.

A turning point came when MacDonald's father was unexpectedly fired in 1947 during Vancouver mayor Gerry McGeer's overhaul of police personnel following a corruption scandal. "It was the only time I'd ever seen my father cry,"

MacDonald says. "I must have been in about grade ten, and I just remember him coming home very upset. He'd been fired for no reason. In those days the mayor could fire anybody, and there was no labour relations board to fight it. But Gordon Scott, who was the city prosecutor at the time, resigned over McGeer's campaign, and they had to hire everyone back. My father had to start over as a patrol constable again, but he was back in the job he loved. McGeer died in office later that same year."

MacDonald joined the VPD in 1956. "There were a lot of things different on the job then," he says. "The training took about three months, and then they gave you a gun and handcuffs and told you to go catch crooks. That was better than no training at all, but the technology and tools of the trade were so different from today. Back then, it was state of the art to have a little panel on the bottom corner of the windshield that you could push out in case you needed to shoot out the tires of a car you were chasing, though it's not as though that happened often—or that everybody was a good enough shot to do it!"

McDonald moved through different sections of the police department to eventually be assigned as staff sergeant to head a re-formation of the vice squad in 1975. This consolidated the separate liquor, gambling, and morality squads under a new organizational umbrella: the "general vice" squad. "It was the old Protestant ethic when they considered everything not nice was terrible!" McDonald jokes.

The new VPD vice squad mandate wasn't popular with veteran detectives. "A lot of them operated independently as their own experts in their field," MacDonald says. "And to tell you the truth, most of them were. You had guys like Harry Walters, who was an expert in gambling and bookmaking cases. He would get called to testify in court as an expert in illegal gambling cases—I didn't need to instruct him to do anything he didn't know already. There were so many first-class people to work with. And I couldn't wait to get to work a little early and stay a little late. We had fun. So to a lot of people, I just said, 'Don't worry about me, just go ahead and do your job.'"

The new general vice squad was supervised by Inspector Ken Brown, with McDonald left to manage the team of six detectives from the gambling squad, eight from the morality squad, and two from the liquor squad. To supplement their numbers as needed, the division had access to patrol and undercover officers, as well as crime prevention units like the kind Gord Bader and Al Robson were on.

When McDonald started his police career in the 1950s, the sex trade in the West End was known for being discreet. "You had a few call girls working out of the West End, but they kept it low-key. But by the 1970s, it had become such a public issue it took up a lot of police time," he recalls.

It was to supervisors like McDonald and Brown that Detective Jim Maitland and others on the general vice squad presented the plan to expand the investigation of Wayne Harris with a wiretap on Harris's telephone.

Today, phone records and recordings of calls—whether on landlines or cellphones—can be accessed using extremely sophisticated digital telecommunication. But in the 1970s, the assignment was a far more low-tech affair. It was also by no means a new process. Police departments had been able to monitor phone calls in decades previous, when the procedure was as straightforward as having an officer who knew what he was doing climb up a telephone pole and jump a connection. For many years there were next to no legal requirements for warrants—it only meant the information couldn't be used in court.

"There was a sergeant in the drug squad in the early 1950s named Blackie MacDonald—he was a real genius," says Staff Sergeant Glenn MacDonald, no relation. "He'd built a telephone—it looked like a bulky mobile phone—that could be attached to a phone line from outside, and it would count and record the clicks that the old rotary phones made as somebody dialed the number. So you would count by those clicks the telephone number they were calling, then find out later through the phone company reverse directory who they were calling."

By the 1970s, with so many in the West End living in apartment buildings, it was no longer as easy as it had been twenty years earlier to tap into an exterior telephone wire. Still, it was not uncommon for police officers to have master keys to telephone utility rooms in apartment buildings, which granted direct access to the junction box for the whole building.

Officers like Al Robson took street-level surveillance more seriously than most. "There used to be these sheets they posted at headquarters called Form 19s that listed officers observations on some places and areas that they had seen on their shift the day or night before. A lot of people didn't pay much attention to those sheets, but I always had a look at them. When I had a break, I'd go down and observe one of the houses or apartment buildings listed on the Form 19 for fifteen or twenty minutes, and sometimes I'd catch what was going on—a drug deal, or something," Robson says.

"I let the dealers rat on themselves," Robson says with a wry smile. "We didn't arrest the low-level addicts, and you could never make an arrest on gossip. I just found out who people were buying from higher up. But it was really the drug dealers turning themselves in—or they'd have information that would lead to bigger things."

Robson recalls an incident in which a dealer he arrested, and who became one of his informants, revealed that two men were planning an armed bank robbery. He notified his supervisors, and a team staked out the suspects' home to catch them in the act. But after three days, the suspects hadn't left.

"[The surveillance team] called me up and said, 'We're going to wrap up the stakeout,' because nothing had happened for three days. So I told them, 'Let me talk to my rat and call you back.' I knew they were going to do the bank robbery, so I waited an hour and called them back and told them to wait one more day. Sure enough, they'd tried to rob the next day and they got caught. Informants and tipsters got a $500 reward for a tip on a bank holdup—so I'd give that to the informant I knew. He'd buy a bundle of heroin for it, keep some for himself, and tell me who he bought it from. Weeks later, once things had cooled down so the informant wouldn't be connected to it, I'd go after them and move up the chain. It worked like a successful pyramid scheme."

Robson netted so many serious criminal arrests from street-level surveillance and informants that he got word from officials that his network was the best of any young constable on the VPD.

With the investigation into Wayne Harris approved by VPD superintendents, it would fall under the purview of Maitland's team in the vice squad to supervise the wiretaps. Robson and Bader would remain as key investigators, but the broader investigation added police officers Ian Hay and Trish Raymond, as well as senior detectives George Hake and Ken Johnstone.[13] Hake and Johnstone had joined the VPD in the 1950s and been involved in sex trade investigations and, in 1983, the seizure of X-rated material from two locations of the adult rental chain Red Hot Video.

The focus of the Harris investigation was a wiretap on the telephone at Wayne and Helga Harris's apartment, a second-floor suite as 2358 York Avenue in Kitsilano. Calls coming in and going out were monitored at the headquarters of the CLEU—Coordinated Law Enforcement Unit—just over six kilometres

---

[13] Hay, Hake, and Johnstone are deceased, and Raymond declined to be interviewed for this book.

away at 250 West 7th Avenue near Mount Pleasant. CLEU was formed just three years earlier, in 1974, after the provincial Attorney General's office observed that British Columbia's crime rate had more than doubled from 1962 to 1971. The AG's office determined that crime in the Lower Mainland needed to be addressed as a whole by one body, rather than fractionally between the fiefdoms of so many different city police and RCMP detachments.

The wiretapping technology wasn't much different from the days of Blackie MacDonald. "You'd hear on the recording the click of the [rotary] phone, so you could slow down the tape to hear the number of clicks as the number was dialed and write that down," Bader says. Telephone conversations from the Harris home phone were recorded on large audiotape reels, Bader recalls, which could be played back later by investigators like him and Robson. While officers were out in the field, police interns or volunteers, who were often police academy trainees, could listen live as the recordings were being made. If a wiretapped suspect called someone to say they were leaving for a meeting, the intern could notify police in the field in real time that a suspect was on the move. Sitting and listening, waiting for the calls, could be a tedious affair. Moreover, the police often didn't have the personnel necessary for twenty-four-hour surveillance. Sometimes they could only listen to recordings after the fact.

The Harris wiretap investigation continued through early 1977. The audiotapes have long since been discarded or destroyed, as have many police files, which outside of major crimes like homicides are largely expunged after twenty-five to thirty years. As a result, researchers are left mostly with the memories of the police officers themselves as the only remaining resource for information on investigations.

Harris suspected police were watching him, though Bader remembers that Harris was by no means a criminal mastermind. "I remember one of the wiretap phone calls where Harris had one of the kids he had under his wing asking if he had any weed," says Bader. "He told the kid, 'Don't say that word over the phone, man'—next time when you call, ask for *beer*.' Well, the kid called back a couple of days later and said, "Hey Wayne, I was going to come over and grab some beer off you,' and Wayne replied, 'Beer? I don't have any beer. What are you talking about?' Harris was clueless as to what he'd told the kid."

Robson recalls the wiretap revealed some of what Helga Harris was up to. She and a friend were talking about being a duo at a bachelor party. This presented a hurdle for the investigative team because police surveillance rules required if they were made aware of a crime that was going to take place, they had to try to stop it. But intercepting the women at the party could potentially blow the vice squad's cover.

The quandary was resolved on the night of the gathering when police showed up midway through. As they detained Helga, her friend, and the bachelor party attendees, the officers made overt announcements that one of the unnamed guests had talked too loudly and specifically about the planned activities, and that's how police got wise. Despite Wayne and Helga's suspicion that their phone was being tapped, the secrecy of the police surveillance detail remained intact.

"One of the names that came up early in the investigation was Hal Keller," Jim Maitland says.

Born in Vienna, Keller had gone to university in Edmonton, where he had also worked as an accountant. Later, he was a sales tax auditor for the federal government. He moved to Vancouver, and in 1972, at the age of thirty-two, he borrowed $3,000 from his parents in Texas and started a do-it-yourself picture framing business called U-Frame-It at 1069 Davie Street. The business soon grew into a chain of twenty-three stores across Canada and the US, with retail sales of up to $3 million a year.

"We didn't know who Keller was at first when he and Harris were calling each other," Robson says. "But at one point Keller had contacted Harris about what they called a BYOB party Keller was having, which became very clear wasn't about bringing your own beer but a joke between these chicken hawks about bringing your own boy."

It was difficult to confirm how long Keller had been associated with Harris. Their dealings had previously gone undetected because of the anonymity of the adolescents involved. These were street kids and runaways who lived on the fringes of society away from parental and institutional oversight, which seemed to allow Harris to keep his operation discreet. The wiretap revealed that some of the adolescents were from other parts of Canada and the US, and although some may have travelled on their own between cities, others may have been trafficked. The wiretap elevated police concerns that Harris was acting as a pimp and introducing young boys, aged twelve to seventeen, to Keller and what appeared to be other, often wealthy men in the city.

Keller's home was at 4447 West 2nd Avenue, just south of Jericho Beach in West Point Grey. Today, this neighbourhood is home to Vancouver's most expensive multi-million-dollar mansions. Even in 1977, before the city experienced its post–Expo 86 real estate boom, Point Grey was regarded as an area for the city's most wealthy and influential residents—lawyers, financial managers, politicians. It was hardly the kind of location where Bader and Robson were used to setting up a stakeout. Just two months earlier, they were staking out public toilets, and now they found themselves surveilling an upscale home in one of the city's most affluent neighbourhoods.

"We sat on the house for a while watching people arrive and leave that night," Robson says. "There were young boys arriving there, in the company of what was obviously older men. We took down licence plate numbers and tried to get a closer look inside the house, but it was difficult to see inside from the street. I walked around outside, but the fences were high, and even from the back alley you couldn't get close to any windows without really easily being given away and spotted. Today, it might have even been easier to get an iPhone on a stick and hold it up from under a windowsill, but nobody had anything compact like that then. I tried every way we could to get a better look inside the house, but we just couldn't do it."

U-Frame-It business founder Hal Keller became part of a police investigation in 1977 due to his connections to Wayne Harris.

Vancouver Province Archives

Robson and Maitland say it was difficult to use the conversations between Harris and Keller and others to make criminal convictions unless they were caught in the act with one of the minors. One problem was the wiretap wasn't monitored twenty-four hours a day. On one occasion Maitland says that Keller and

Police charge six in alleged prostitute ring

An unusual influx of young men flashing healthy bankrolls in a downtown area frequented by homosexuals has led police to an alleged prostitution ring involving at least 10 teenage boys and three female prostitutes.

Police said Wednesday the six-month investigation and the charging of six alleged ringleaders directing the boys was bolstered by calls from parents and relatives concerned over marked mental and physical changes in the boys.

Police say they also received reports that boys, aged 12 to 16, were given drugs such as hashish and marijuana, provided in some cases with board and lodging and were given money for engaging in prostitution with men.

Det. Jim Maitland said Wednesday that most of the boys involved have socially disrupted backgrounds, some coming from one-parent homes. He said the boys were put under observation to ascertain their alleged "employers."

"These boys are frequently found to be in possesion of and to be spending considerable quantities of money," he said.

Charged with conspiracy to live off the avails of prostitution, keeping a common bawdy house, gross indecency and contributing to juvenile delinquency are: Wayne Harris, 29; his wife Joanne Harris, 22; Roger Longtin, 17; Robert Boston, 21; Ray Paris, 31 and Denis Harton, 34.

After months of investigation and wiretapping, the VPD filed charges against Wayne Harris and his prostitution ring.

another man had raped one youth so violently that the victim had to be taken discreetly for emergency medical attention from a private doctor. Members of the vice squad were pained by the details—especially since they couldn't do anything about it. "By the time Bader and Robson came on duty to listen to the wire, they were probably two hours too late to catch the people in the act," Maitland says.

"Part of the problem was we were never given the manpower to properly investigate the whole thing," Robson says. "While we were assigned to investigate, it never had the priority that it would have probably been given today. And at the time, we didn't have a full idea until later of how many people were involved and who they were."

On April 12, 1977, though, the investigation came to a head. Wayne Harris was finally charged with living off the avails of prostitution, keeping a common bawdy house, conspiracy, contributing to juvenile delinquency, and gross indecency. Ray Paris and Helga Harris were arrested for similar charges, as police had determined that they were directly involved in sex with the minors. Three other suspects who were believed to be accomplices were also arrested.

"When the police came into Harris's apartment," Robson recalls, "they found Helga there in the middle of turning a trick while Harris was in the shower. Harris came out of the shower to find his apartment full of police. At the best of times, Harris could be pretty surly and sarcastic, and he was pretty lippy about being arrested."

Reports of the arrest were relegated to the back pages of newspapers. Interviewed for the *Province,* Maitland stated that the ring had involved female and teenage male sex workers. He said the boys had come from "socially disrupted backgrounds," though not all were runaways who weren't cared for. The investigation had been "bolstered by calls from parents and relatives concerned over marked mental and physical changes in the boys," Maitland said. Some of the parents also noticed the kids had much more cash than teenagers would typically possess. Police determined that Harris had coerced or intimidated some of the adolescents he oversaw. Of those who worked for Harris, few of them are either alive or could be found. The one who was contacted chose not to be interviewed for this book. Local television newscasts didn't provide much coverage either. The story would have probably garnered wider attention had some of the names of the clients connected to the Harris ring been publicized—and not just Hal Keller's. Names that would have been known to the public in Vancouver and in fact across Canada. But those would remain secret for much longer.

Three associates of Wayne and Helga Harris and Ray Paris were also named in the charges. Seventeen-year-old Roger Longtin had started out as one of Wayne Harris's sex workers, but police believed that Longtin had also recruited other young men for Harris and shared in the profits. Thirty-four-year-old Denis Harton was later convicted of trafficking cocaine, but it remains unclear how he was connected with Harris. Both had their charges in the Harris investigation dropped before the case went to trial.

The last person named was twenty-one-year-old Robert Boston. Al Robson recalls that police believed that Boston was only involved in the theft aspects of the Harris crime ring. Boston, now sixty-five, claims he has no idea why he was arrested.

Boston had worked as a doorman and bouncer at various nightclubs in Vancouver, including the Dance Machine and the Thunderbird Club. To him, Harris was little more than an acquaintance—someone he saw regularly in Vancouver's nightlife scene. "Wayne hung around at a lot of the clubs I was at," Boston says. "It was one of those things—people would leave a message for him, or somebody would ask me if I saw him, and I passed some messages if I talked to him on the phone. I'd been at his home two or three times to smoke a joint. I knew Helga was pretty much what you'd call a steady working girl back then, but I had no idea what was going on."

The Dance Machine was a frequent haunt for Harris. An after-hours club located at 887 Seymour, next to the Orpheum theatre, it didn't have a liquor licence, but that didn't stop patrons from bringing in their own bottles—or drugs. "We'd open at midnight and close around seven a.m.," says Boston. "There were more drugs around there than you could shake a huge stick at. I remember a guy who came into the club who was selling whole ounces of MDMA there. But the whole city was different. Back in those days you could walk down Davie Street and buy everything from speed to coke, Mandrax, and MDMA."

Boston says that he found out after the charges that Harris's phone had been tapped and wondered if the nature of his telephone calls had made him a suspect. "I had a bit of an attitude about authority back then, so maybe it was something I said on the phone. We had a pretty good relationship overall at the club, but I never saw what Wayne was up to back then. I was completely surprised—he kept that part of his life hidden, it seems. I knew he had an eye for boys, and rumour was that he was not averse to forcing himself on people—and let's just say that none of that was my side of the street."

Charges against Boston were also dropped before the trial.

A week prior to charges being filed against Harris, the VPD hosted a community meeting at the West End Community Centre. The auditorium had a capacity of 200 people, and police anticipated that roughly 50 people would attend. Instead, nearly 400 people packed the auditorium that night. In attendance was a broad mix of conservative older residents, students, gay activists, and, as the *Vancouver Sun* described them, "garishly dressed prostitutes." These engaged citizens filled every seat and sat on every inch of floor available, while others listened from doorways. The event turned out to be one of the most raucous community meetings in the history of the West End.

Representing the VPD were Inspector Doug Westover, in charge of District One, which included all of the West End; Staff Sergeant Glenn MacDonald, head of the general vice squad; and Staff Sergeant Harvey Brown. Had the police administrators known the meeting would descend into chaos, they might have called in a few riot squad members to keep order as well.

The April 1977 town hall–style meeting of West End residents brought out a wide array of speakers.

Also present were the two police officers who perhaps had come to know the West End streets better than anyone on the force: constables Gord Bader and Al Robson. They didn't want to be there. It wasn't that they didn't care, but these kinds of community outreach initiatives didn't suit their personalities and demeanour. Robson had scanned the room when the event began and recognized the faces of about a dozen individuals that he'd arrested over the years—for everything from soliciting to drug possession. Many of these individuals, in turn, recognized him. Most met Robson's wry smile with looks of defiant antipathy.

This meeting had been organized in response to mounting complaints from West End residents who demanded police action to address the noise and late-night disruption they felt was a result of the sex trade occurring in the neighbourhood, specifically along the 1000 to 1200 blocks of Davie Street. After some standard opening remarks from senior police, several in attendance complained about how the sex workers who walked the streets and the cruising johns who solicited them.

One female resident said she was sick of being harassed each time she walked down the street by those who assumed she was a sex worker. A common question to neighbourhood women from drivers on the prowl was "You walkin' or workin'?" This woman suggested that if the police didn't take action to protect residents soon, it would be too late and someone would be attacked.

Other speakers came forward. "Speaking for the prostitutes," the *Vancouver Sun* noted, "was a dark-haired woman wearing a revealingly low-cut blouse, who said that the prostitutes had to group together in a small area to protect themselves from harassment," and that "prostitutes would sooner do their work quietly and not bother anyone," but it was the police who corralled them into certain areas. Another woman shot back that she "didn't care what they did, as long as they didn't do it under their window—and why couldn't they conduct their business across the street where there was no apartment building?" According to the *Vancouver Sun,* this comment garnered significant applause.

Some of the most vocal speakers that night were members of the Gay Alliance Toward Equality (GATE), who charged that police called the meeting to manipulate public sentiment in support of an intensified campaign against gay people—they even questioned what legal right police had to call the meeting in the first place.

GATE members distributed to those assembled leaflets that read:

> Gays Will Not Be Scapegoated. Davie Street is unpleasant. However, gays and other people there are not responsible for this state of affairs when human relations are reduced to buy and sell and competition. Gays have no control over Davie Street. Gay people go there to socialize because we have few alternatives in an anti-gay society. Poor women are forced to sell their bodies in order to survive, and high unemployment, especially among youth, drives young men to prostitution. Those city officials and developers who self-righteously wring their hands are themselves the ones who have created Davie St. through distorted priorities which put real estate profits ahead of human need.

GATE (Gay Alliance Toward Equality) protesters take over the stage behind police at the West End Community Centre.

Two members of GATE felt the leaflets weren't enough. Don Hann and Rob Joyce marched to the stage with a banner to stand behind seated police officials. "We didn't plan in advance to take the stage," recalls Hann, who still lives in Vancouver. "Police weren't prepared for the avalanche of questions being thrown at them and didn't expect that militancy. But it was really because of the way the police responded to the questions that it felt like symbolically taking the stage meant we were saying to police, 'What we're hearing from you is unconvincing.'"

Staff Sergeant Glenn MacDonald gave a brief talk concerning police activities against sex work, but he was cut short by a gay man who protested that he had been arrested at English Bay for "doing something which if it had been a member of the opposite sex would have been totally overlooked." Other gay men took the microphone and shared anecdotes of police harassment, like when, just days earlier, the police had raided several gay nightclubs and made more than thirty arrests for drugs like amyl nitrate and marijuana (both still regarded at the time as contraband by the drug squad).

When MacDonald insisted that the vice squad didn't target gay men, he was rigorously jeered at by the crowd. To a degree, MacDonald was correct—the VPD had no standing orders to target the gay community. But to those present,

MacDonald was ignoring the wealth of anecdotal evidence of individual officers who were harassing gay men or making prejudicial comments about them during police stops.

"Individual officers can be the ones culpable at the end of the day," Don Hann says. "But GATE wrote a letter to the chief of police asking that a directive be issued forbidding individual officers from expressing negative views about gays in the course of duty. The chief refused."

As the evening wore on, the meeting dissolved into chaos. One audience member repeatedly stated he hadn't come to the meeting to listen to "a bunch of creampuffs," and another, annoyed by the GATE banner at the front of the room, called for the activists to be "kicked off" the stage. People began to shout insults and threats at one another. A shoving match broke out at the back of the hall and participants had to be separated. Inspector Westover apologized to those in attendance who came to discuss noise problems, noting, ironically, "Unfortunately, you've been drowned out by others who came here to use this meeting for their own purposes."

"The whole thing started out well intentioned enough," Robson recalls. "People were civil and passing around the mic saying that as residents they couldn't sleep with all the noise of the johns coming and going, screaming in the alleyways, used condoms being left everywhere, but the whole thing descended into disorder when the guys with the banner got up behind Westover. From then on, every single group and subgroup was just concerned with making their own point. I put my head down, and I just wanted to slink out of there. It almost turned into a little riot." Acting chief Ted Oliver conveyed regret in his comments to the *Province* afterward: "Each group didn't listen to the other. There was no communication."[14]

Residents who had come to the meeting to complain about neighbourhood noise and disruption eventually found a platform. Their sentiments were conveyed— this time loud and clear—in a *Vancouver Sun* feature by Carol Volkart, published a week later. Volkart, who had attended the community meeting, had observed Davie Street for a few hours on a typical night from the third-floor corner unit in the Capitola Apartments at 1209 Thurlow Street. She documented street fights, cars cruising up and down Davie catcalling passersby, loud conversations, and sex workers getting in and out of cars along the street with regularity. "Through the morning, the traffic noise was so loud and so continual that little street conversation could be heard above it ... whoops, shouts, and wolf-whistles from

[14] "Davie Street Meet 'Was Not a Success,'" *Vancouver Province*, April 7, 1977.

Vancouver Sun Archives

The *Vancouver Sun*'s Carol Volkart overlooking Davie Street at Thurlow. For a 1977 article, Volkart reported on a "typical night on Davie Street" that underscored how disruptive many felt the street had become.

merry-makers rose even above the high-decibel level. The flow of traffic was continuous from midnight until about 3 a.m."[15]

But the anger West End residents expressed at the meeting at the community centre and the news reports about just how uncomfortable they felt in their own neighbourhood was only the half of it. The worst was yet to come.

[15] Carol Volkart, "Prostitutes, Gays Clash with Residents," *Vancouver Sun*, April 7, 1977, 27.

CHAPTER 7

The Fire This Time

It was a hot summer evening on July 30, 1977, when Gord Bader and Al Robson once again found themselves hiding out doing surveillance. This night they were in a parking lot on the east side of the 1000 block of Seymour Street, just across the street from the Penthouse Nightclub.

It had been a hot summer and a particularly eventful one around town. The city's first SeaBus, which ferried foot passengers between downtown and the North Shore, had started running a month earlier. Harbour Centre, the tallest building in Vancouver at the time, at 147 metres (482 feet), opened and immediately became a defining landmark in the city's skyline. In cinemas, the latest James Bond movie, *The Spy Who Loved Me*, starring Roger Moore as Agent 007, had just opened, and on the radio, Steve Miller Band's "Jet Airliner" dominated the rock 'n' roll airwaves. The mysterious and ominous Son of Sam shootings that terrorized the outer boroughs of New York was making news across North America, though such heinous, big-city criminal acts still seemed alien and remote to most Vancouverites, who fervently believed "it couldn't happen here."

With the arrest of Wayne Harris and his associates in April that year and the court case pending, Bader and Robson were no longer directly involved with the vice investigation. They were happy to move on from the investigation of chicken hawks and hustlers, to put the long hours of listening to wiretaps behind them, and to be back on the streets downtown.

"That summer, around the Penthouse and down to the old Arts Club building [1181 Seymour Street], there had been a lot of theft from automobiles," Robson says. "So I decided one night to sacrifice my own car—I had a '69 Mustang Grande, 351 Cleveland engine, that I parked in the lot there. I left the windows partially down—it was my version of a bait car. I was praying somebody would break into it. I was farther away from the car, hiding behind a Cadillac, keeping an eye on the whole parking lot, but I wasn't worried. Gord was close enough, and fast enough, that if somebody tried to break into it or steal it, he could chase after them like a cheetah and bite like a lion if there was any problem."

For an hour or so nothing happened. Both men sat on the ground keeping an eye on Robson's car, as traffic along Seymour Street could be heard passing by, occasionally checking in with each another over their police radios. Robson joked that, considering how warm the evening was, waiting might have been more enjoyable if they had a cold six-pack of beer to share.

Then Robson saw smoke coming out of the window of an old rooming house behind him at 1044 Seymour Street. Suddenly, the sound of breaking glass pierced the quiet evening as a windowpane shattered and shards fell to the ground. Flames burst out of the window as the curtains caught fire.

"Gord, did you see that?" Robson called to his partner on the radio.

"Yeah!" Bader shouted back.

Robson radioed dispatch: "Car 50—we've got a huge fire across the street from the Penthouse, in an old rooming house here!"

Bader had a head start and was already on running to the house. Reaching the front door first, Bader flung it open and Robson was stunned to see him run in without hesitation. Robson had seen fires in old wooden houses before. The shake roofs went up in flames like kindling. He yelled to Bader from the front door as he crossed the threshold, peering into the house. He could taste the smoke.

Bader was already on his way out, carrying a severely burned man. He bumped into Robson, pushing them both out the door. The smell of burning flesh might have doubled them over if the smoke from the fire had not overwhelmed them.

"[The man] had begun what we used to call pugilizing," Robson says. "In severe burns, the contraction of the muscles causes joints to flex and take a boxer's stance, with the elbows and fists clenched. I had already inhaled so much smoke I coughed into that dying man's face on the ground, and he's grabbing my face—I'll never forget it."

Picking himself up, Robson yelled into his police radio. "Code 4! Emergency! Man in trouble! Police in trouble! This whole place is ablaze! Where is the fire department?!" Before Robson knew it, Bader had run back into the burning house to help another occupant who was already on his way out. This man was relatively uninjured, aside from some smoke inhalation. Bader turned around and again ran into the house before Robson could call him back.

Bader bounded up to the second floor of the house. Smoke was now at his shoulders, so he crouched as he ran down a hallway, opening doors and finding empty rooms until, at last, he found another man. "The house is on fire—you gotta get out of here!" Bader barked at him. The man had been asleep. He bolted upright and Bader ran into the room to grab him. The man was only in his undershorts, so he threw on some pants, and then started looking around the room.

"What the hell are you waiting for? We gotta go!" Bader shouted. The roar of the fire could now be heard in the lower section of the building and only seemed to be getting louder.

"I'm looking for my wallet!" the man replied.

"To hell with that!" Bader shouted, and grabbed him by the waist, leading him to the top of the stairs down to the main floor of the house. By now the smoke was coming in thick and fast. The men crouched so low, they were practically on their hands and knees.

"When an old wooden house burns, it isn't simply the furniture or drapery that's making all that smoke but the floor coverings, the vinyl, the nylon," Bader says. "It produces these chemicals that with the smoke it feels like somebody is pouring acid down your throat. By the time I got to the stairs, I couldn't see anything, and I started yelling for Al."

In the panic and fear of the moment, Robson felt he couldn't enter the house as Bader had. He stood at the doorway as smoke billowed out, hearing glass breaking upstairs, and then a *boom*—the sound of something inside the house collapsing.

"Gord! Gord! For Christ's sake!" he screamed into the house. Robson couldn't see anything inside; it was pitch-black. But he heard Bader yelling. He couldn't hear over the roar of the fire if any sirens were coming to help. But he could hear Bader. Robson drew as big a breath as he could and ran inside.

Even when he crouched down, Robson couldn't see anything. The smoke was too dark and thick. Drawn to the sound of Bader's shouting, he climbed the stairs, grabbing for anything he could. He couldn't believe it when his hand found Bader through the smoke. Robson pulled on Bader, who pulled on the man he'd found on the top floor, and the three rolled down the stairs and practically right out the front door.

A fire truck finally pulled up, and a crew mobilized to extinguish the fire that had enveloped one side of the house. Bader and Robson, along with the two surviving rescued men finally had a chance to catch their breath.

Retelling the story almost forty-five years later, Robson, for all his hard-boiled exterior, is still in awe. "I have no problem with dead bodies at all," he says.

"It was just the bravado of Gordie. I've done a lot of stupid things running into places without any fear, but that was the bravest thing I ever saw in my life. He pulled one body out and then another. It was like a meat factory."

Robson felt Bader's bravery shouldn't go unnoticed, so he sent a commendation to the chief. On August 24, 1977, both men were honoured for their display of personal courage. Robson felt uncomfortable accepting the commendation. He felt he hadn't done anything to earn it—Bader had been the only one of merit. But Bader recalls, "When they asked me about it, I said, 'Look, Al saved my ass by pulling me out of there.'"

The incident barely made local news reports and is only mentioned in a list of accidental deaths from that weekend—forty-three-year-old Gerald Francis Rogers, who had suffered burns over ninety-five percent of his body, had died in a house fire, with the cause unknown but suspected to have started as a mattress fire caused by a lit cigarette. There was no news on the two survivors or of the efforts of the two cops who had rescued them. The commendations from the VPD also went unreported.

All these years later, Bader is remarkably detached from the severity of the incident. "It's a strange job being a cop. You get paid to arrest some people and save others. I actually don't remember that night as much as Al does for some reason. Maybe my mind just kicked in—it seems crazy to think about it now. But there were a lot of days and nights like that back then, as well as nights where absolutely nothing happened. I guess it was just another night on the job."

After a few days off following the Seymour Street house fire, Bader and Robson returned to duty, surprised to find that they had once again been deployed to the West End. Two other regular vice squad officers in the area, George Stern and Vic Farmer, would be on holiday for about week, and Bader and Robson were directed to fill in.

Stern and Farmer had been partners in the VPD for more than ten years and had worked in the West End for some time. Farmer would go on to become one of the senior polygraphists in the department in the 1980s. But, on this particular beat, it became apparent to Bader and Robson that Farmer and Stern had seemingly been so busy dealing with female street sex workers and trying to appease residential complaints that they hadn't investigated the street hustler scene along Davie.

In August 1977, while filling in on this West End patrol, Bader and Robson were joined for a ride-along by Marcus Gee, a twenty-two-year-old newspaper reporter who was writing an article on sex work in the West End. Gee was in his fourth year at the University of British Columbia, working during summer break as a reporter for the *Province*. This was a time when daily newspapers hired writers from local universities to handle city beats and crime reporting. "It was probably my second summer working for the paper, and it was probably my first or second ride-along that I'd ever done with any police," Gee recalls today from Toronto, where he is an award-winning urban affairs columnist for the *Globe and Mail*.

Over the course of that warm August evening, with Robson driving and Bader in the passenger seat, Gee sat in the back of the patrol car as they did their rounds up and down Davie Street. The cops told Gee about the six-month investigation into Wayne Harris (though they didn't identify him by name). They cruised past some of the late-night downtime hangouts for sex workers. Past Davie and Thurlow by the Bino's restaurant, to the Pizza Patio at Davie and Bute, and down to English Bay. Doubling back, they spotted Mark, the young hustler who had first told them about Harris almost a year earlier. By this point, Robson and Bader had developed an amicable relationship with Mark. He had become a good source of information and street gossip. Robson called him over to their car. Mark recognized them and approached in an exaggerated sashay, causing an eruption of laughter and wolf whistles from Mark's friends and passersby along the street corner.

"I told Mark that Gee was a reporter and wanted to talk to him," Robson says. "So we drove around while Gee had his tape recorder out. And Mark wouldn't stop talking, telling him about what was going on out there." Mark described what an average night was like for him. He would usually turn tricks in one of the West End alleyways. He'd be treated well some nights; on others he'd have some of bad dates—occasionally, there'd be those who would threaten to kill him when he protested their refusal to pay. "Some guys who are into S-M like to hit me with belts and whips and stuff, but it usually doesn't hurt much. I don't mind," Mark told Gee.

Bader and Robson provided background for Gee. They told him that many of the youth working the streets in the West End had been reported as missing persons in other parts of Canada and the US, and when they were arrested for prostitution some were flown or bused back home at the family's expense. Others worked their way back on their own. Mark estimated that most of the couple of hundred kids he thought to be involved in the Vancouver street hustling scene were aged fourteen to seventeen, but there were some as young as twelve.

"Boy, Gee's eyes were like saucers by the time we got finished," Bader recalls. "After he'd heard from Mark about all these orgies and kinky sex, the chicken hawks, the money, and how prevalent it all was, he couldn't believe it. Al and I had a pretty good idea of what was going on by then, and we'd been dealing with it for a year, so it wasn't as much of a shock to us, but to Gee—he was just stunned by it all."

Robson eventually dropped Mark off at his corner. They continued to drive around for another hour, introducing Gee to some other hustlers they'd gotten to know over the past several months, before they wrapped up for the night. Robson asked Gee to show him the story before it ran.

"I don't remember a lot about that night. It was so many years ago," Gee says cautiously. "But I do remember how surprised I was about it all. It was just so open in the streets."

Bader and Robson might have forgotten the night as well, if it weren't for the fallout when Gee's story "Boy Prostitutes Moving Onto Davie Street Corners" ran in the Saturday, August 13, 1977, issue of the *Province* newspaper. Gee quoted some of the details Bader and Robson gave from their past nine months of work in the West End. Wayne Harris was never named, but aspects of the investigation that led to his arrest were described. And it was made clear that, despite the arrest, these problems persisted in the West End.

Gee also quoted some of the more shocking details of Mark's life on the streets, including the fact that chicken hawks had become bolder about seeking out young men like him, who were making $30 to $40 a trick, and often up to $200 a night doing sex work and posing for pornographic photos or films.

Gee had interviewed Detective Jim Maitland, who confirmed there was little police could do to keep the young men from hustling, aside from speaking with them directly or referring them to social agencies. "Child welfare agencies try to send the boys home," Maitland said, "but they seldom succeed. They put the kids on the bus, and they get off at the next stop and are on the street again the next day."

Gee suggested that police were fearful of someone getting killed—invoking what would become a notorious criminal incident in Toronto that had occurred just weeks before, when twelve-year-old shoeshine boy Emanuel Jaques was lured with the promise of money for some odd jobs but was instead raped and killed in what Gee misguidedly described as "a homosexual orgy."

A controversial August 1977 *Vancouver Province* exposé on West End street prostitution caused a backroom firestorm for the VPD—and for Gord Bader and Al Robson, who had escorted *Province* reporter Marcus Gee on the ride-along.

Gee also reported that "Robson and Bader are trying to fight the problem by working with Vancouver's gay community, which is very concerned about the situation," and that the pair were developing contacts with people in the community who might be able to dissuade the boys from hustling. However, this was another situation in which those involved in child exploitation were simply labelled as "homosexuals," rather than called out as pederasts and pedophiles. Gee's language was not dissimilar from much of the reporting on the issue at the time. This damaging kind of characterization of the gay community as a whole would be perpetuated for years.

The details of Gee's article were too shocking and salacious for the syndicated western Canadian newspapers to ignore. The story also ran in city newspapers from Edmonton to Saskatoon, with new headlines like "Vancouver's Homosexual 'Chicken Trade' Shocks City," suggesting to the western half of the country that Vancouver had become a den of perversion. There was no way the news stories would go unnoticed. Early the following Monday morning, Bader and Robson got telephone calls at their homes that they should come in early before their afternoon shift. The chief of police himself, Don Winterton, wanted to speak to them.

Neither man had seen the weekend news story until they were shown a newspaper clipping before they headed into the chief's office. Robson was immediately angry that Gee hadn't sent him the article before it ran. Gee says he doesn't recall Robson asking to review the article before it ran, but Robson is adamant he made such a request. Gee does remember that there was "some pushback" from police for the article's estimate of 200 male sex workers, even though that number had been confirmed by the report prepared by UBC's Monique Layton two years earlier on sex work in Vancouver. Now Mayor Jack Volrich and other city officials were being questioned about the figures cited in the article and being asked to comment on why the mayor and police department were unaware of them.

The firestorm of media attention over Gee's article is largely forgotten, and the issue of underage male sex workers is often overlooked when it comes to the subject of the West End sex trade in the 1970s and early '80s. There is only one sentence about the story in Daniel Francis's otherwise very detailed 2006 book *Red Light Neon: A History of Vancouver's Sex Trade,* and Stan Persky's 1980 book *The House That Jack Built: Mayor Jack Volrich and Vancouver Politics* largely dismisses the article as newspaper sensationalism—claiming that "the Monday morning police reaction was a lazy yawn," with the VPD broadly promising the public that the vice squad would fully investigate.

But Bader and Robson were hardly greeted with a yawn when they arrived to speak to the chief at VPD headquarters that morning.

Waiting for them in the office, along with Chief Winterton, were three other inspectors: Ted Oliver, Bob Stewart, and Mike Farren. "Farren started in on us first—nobody ever liked him," Robson says, imitating Farren's Irish accent: "'Jaysus Christ—have you two read the news? Do you know how much trouble you're in!? Where didja get these numbers about 200 boy hookers!?' Well, he went at us for a while, saying the mayor was furious about it—what hadn't they been told?" The other supervisors looked on stoically.

"Then Gord, completely unexpectedly, piped up—'Why is it every time the mayor gets his head in a twist, you guys run around with your heads cut off?' Goddammit, I thought we were done for—on desk or jail duty for a year," Robson says. "I just wanted to sink into my shoes and disappear."

"Yeah, I guess I'd had enough," Bader laughs. "But that's what it was like back then. These guys didn't know what we were dealing with in the streets, and what we'd just been doing for months with the investigation into Harris. They were always dealing with the fallout or politics of a fire after the fact."

It was left to Chief Winterton to bring the escalating meeting to order. "All right, here's what's going to happen," Robson recalls him saying. "Starting this week, you two are going to go out there with a couple of other vice officers, and you prove to me that there are 200 hustlers out there. That's it."

Vancouver Sun Archives

Two adolescent male sex workers on a West End street, circa late 1970s.

There wasn't much left to say. Dismissed, Bader and Robson left the chief's office, dejected. They'd just spent the last nine months looking into chicken hawks and hustlers in the West End, hoping that would be the end of it. Now they realized they were headed right back.

The issue of street sex work in the West End continued to be a public concern, with women and trans sex workers garnering most of the press attention. But the article by Marcus Gee brought, at least for the moment, greater focus to the mostly untold stories of male hustlers.

On July 9, 1979, the *Vancouver Sun* ran a profile on one young runaway named Glen, who worked as a hustler independently, without a pimp. He'd been kicked out of his home by his father and hitchhiked from Pembroke, Ontario. His first night in Vancouver, he'd slept in Victory Square downtown, snatched a purse from a pedestrian, and got thirty dollars to pay for a room at the West End YMCA, minutes away from Davie Street where a man propositioned him. As a fifteen-year-old virgin, he turned his first trick.

"I'm not proud of it," Glen told the *Vancouver Sun*. "But I'm young. So what if I put in a few years doing something illegal? I like the people I meet, and the life is neat. If you don't feel like going to work, you don't have to worry about phoning your boss and telling him a lot of lies."[16]

Glen stated that lunch hours, Saturdays, and paydays were the busiest times for male hustlers. The evening trade was unpredictable, depending on how many police were around to slow it down. "You can stand in one place until either a customer or a cop shows up," Glen said. "If a cop shows up first, then you have to move on, or you get charged with loitering. And that's a $15 ticket. But I'm usually lucky and a customer will drive by. If he looks as if he's looking at me I look back at him and smile and wave. If he stops, I go up to the car and say, 'What can I do for you, sir?' The guy will ask me if I'm working, and how much. When he asks me how much, I ask him what he thinks I'm worth. If he says, $20, I'll say 'no, 40,' but it gets me out of the problem of mentioning money first." Thus, Glen would avoid being the instigator of the illegal exchange.

Glen said that most male sex workers charged $40 for oral sex and $75 for anal intercourse. He got the cash up front and refused to take cheques. "A few guys offer cheques, but I tell them they can't go to the bank to get laid." He would consummate the deal in either the customer's home or his own $275-a-month apartment that he shared with his seventeen-year-old girlfriend who had been a sex worker for three years. He said he averaged three or four $40 tricks a night. There was no mention in the story whether condoms were used.

Glen didn't sound like he considered himself to be exploited, but he also didn't see much of a future in this lifestyle. "This experience isn't going to get me anywhere," he said. "But it's a good experience. When I lived at home, I didn't know the first thing about gays or prostitutes, or street life. My parents never told me a thing. We never discussed sex at home. I found out I'm bi-sexual, but I like girls better than I like guys. And if I start saving money, by the time I'm 20 I can go to cooking school and learn to be a chef."

But Glen admitted he was "really loose" with his money and spent a lot on drugs. He considered police crackdowns to be harassment of customers, which ultimately undermined his nightly take. "The streets are crawling with cops now. I even saw some hiding in the bushes the other night."

[16] Kayce White, "Life Is Neat and the Money's Great for the Young Virgin from Pembroke," *Vancouver Sun*, July 9, 1979, 12.

Despite the prominent presence of both sex workers and police in the West End in the 1970s, there was an abiding liberal attitude among many in the community. "At that time there was so much androgynous pop culture everywhere, but that really seemed pronounced in the West End in those years," remembers CBC Radio producer Pamela Post, who grew up in the neighbourhood. "Don't forget this is around the time when David Bowie was first popular, but the West End seemed to show that more than other areas of town. So you saw men holding hands, men wearing dresses walking down Davie Street—the older residents might have turned their heads to look, but most didn't. It all really seemed to be an accepted part of the normal attitude a lot of people had early in the neighbourhood."

Although the West End gained a reputation during the 1960s and '70s for being a progressive and tolerant community, that forbearance did not necessarily extend to the neighbourhood's growing street sex trade. Residents were becoming more vocal in their opposition, and local leaders were aware of their dissent. Across Vancouver, some city officials were always keen to take up the mantle of what they saw as a municipal morality crusade. These hot-button topics ran the gamut from complex social issues, such as sex work, to seemingly more mundane topics, such as public nudity.

For nearly a decade, Vancouverites had been sunning themselves at the city's westernmost stretch of clothing-optional oceanfront known as Wreck Beach. In the summer of 1977, Vancouver alderwoman and Christian evangelist Reverend Bernice Gerard and her group United Citizens for Integrity declared they would "liberate" the beach from the nudists. Gerard remains a vivid figure in city history. With her schoolmarm presence in conservative pantsuit, sensible shoes, and 1940s hairdo, she seemed to be the living embodiment of the *Saturday Night Live* character the Church Lady. Gerard, however, was dead serious, announcing in her unmistakably low voice to listeners of her CJOR radio show that "the nudist takeover alienates this natural paradise from the average citizen."

That summer, Gerard and her followers walked down the UBC bluffs to the shores of Wreck Beach, where they protested what they perceived to be immodesty on display. "No shame!" they called out to the nude sunbathers present and

From protests over nudity at Wreck Beach to Ernie Ruff's van covered in proverbs that drove around the city, concerns about public morality and piety were topical issues in the Vancouver of the 1970s.

offensively declared that "even savages cover their bodies." A group of media photographers were present to capture the stark contrast of this confrontation. The only problem was that the overcast skies that day left Wreck Beach occupied by more of Gerard's followers than naked sun worshippers.

Not all of Vancouver was convinced by Gerard's beachside battle of morality. The *Vancouver Sun* chided, "Forget the silly protest, Miss Gerard. The hole in the knee of your swimsuit is showing."

It's difficult to imagine an openly evangelical Pentecostal preacher like Gerard being elected to city council today. Back then, though, a variety of municipal concerns were being addressed as "moral" issues.

Crusading Seventh-day Adventist Ernie Ruff was someone who saw the changes taking place in Vancouver in moral terms. He felt it was his responsibility to weigh in—not as a politician but as a concerned citizen. For years starting in the mid-1970s, Ruff drove his lumbering A-frame truck covered in passages of apocalyptic Bible verses stacked high above the roof of the cab. He cruised through various neighbourhoods—from Davie Street to the foot of Stanley Park, up through Oakridge and down Broadway like a kind of evangelical ice cream man.

His vehicle trundled along, beseeching citizens to "REPENT AND BE CONVERTED" and "FEAR GOD ... THE HOUR OF HIS JUDGEMENT IS COME."

"Some people think I'm a nut case and throw rocks at me and spit on me," Ruff once told a reporter, adding that persecution of fervent believers was nothing new.

Although he became a very public figure, Ruff's background remained a bit of a mystery. He had led an otherwise quiet life until, after his divorce in the early 1970s, he found himself despondent at the Penthouse Nightclub looking for female company. At this point, he claims that God spoke to him directly in divine intervention, telling him loud and clear that he needed to display scripture on his car and drive around to spread the message.

Ruff lived off small donations from his church and spent a small inheritance on vehicle maintenance, in order to cruise his lumbering truck up and down the streets of Vancouver, his version of Sodom and Gomorrah. He believed people needed to hear the word of God in sin city a lot more than they did on the idyllic BC central coast. Ruff felt time was running out for people, telling told one curious reporter who interviewed him outside his truck. "Huge disasters are coming. So I've got to warn the people."

For at least a few people in our story, he was right.

Davie Street at Howe, 1980.

CHAPTER 8

Framed

An oppressive heat wave weighed down on parts of British Columbia in the summer of 1977. Dry, blistering conditions across the province led to dire forest fires in the Interior. Vancouver experienced sweltering temperatures as well, up to thirty degrees Celsius, but the city became enflamed in a different way.

Although crime in Vancouver had declined overall in the first half of the year, police noted that burglaries and robberies, particularly downtown and in the West End, had gone up—a trend that would continue into the following year, with assaults, auto thefts, sexual offences, and assaults on police officers also increasing. Homicide rates didn't reach anywhere near those of larger American cities, but the twenty-five murders in Vancouver alone (not counting surrounding districts in the Lower Mainland) still gave cause for concern.

Tracking overarching urban crime statistics, though, was not Gord Bader and Al Robson's beat. They were monitoring different stats. In the wake of Marcus Gee's article, they were keeping track of just how many hustlers were active in the city.

"By that time, a lot of the hustlers were congregating around specific places—not just certain streets or corners," says Robson. "But we also went around the bathhouses and massage parlours. We covered so much ground and went into so many sticky places, asking so many questions," Robson says.

One night Robson went into the Playpen South at 1369 Richards Street. The club was one of the more notorious gay nightspots during the period, infamous for the popper-fuelled hedonism of various theme nights. The night that Robson visited the club, a rare evening when he happened to be in uniform, also turned out to be featuring a police theme. The party was in full swing and most patrons simply though his VPD costume looked particularly authentic. Robson managed only a couple of questions to the bartender before some passing revellers pinched his posterior and tried to lead him to the dance floor, before he realized it would be better to come back on another night.

Revellers at a typical night in the Playpen South, remembered as one of the wilder gay nightspots of the late 1970s.

"Within three weeks, we had counted 80 hustlers," says Bader. "While everyone thought that the number was closer to 200, it was just that we didn't manage to find them all. We weren't working every day and night, and we didn't get to finish—we were surprised to be shut down."

Robson, meanwhile, had unexpectedly found himself promoted to corporal. Just six years into his police career, he'd written the exam almost on a lark. At age thirty—considered young for that rank—he was promoted. "They say when you're dumb, they can't fire you—so they promote you," Robson jokes self-deprecatingly. "But to be honest, I didn't think I was due for the promotion."

Robson moved to District Three in South Vancouver to supervise a dozen officers, some of whom were veterans with twenty to thirty years of service. "I won over those old-timers and enjoyed it—later working a bunch of different special squads that focused on armed robberies and breaking-and-entering cases. But I thought about that West End stuff with Gord a lot over the years and how we got thrown into it. While I think we were both glad to move on, there was unfinished business there."

This was part of life for Vancouver police officers. Promotions and transfers after a term would mean new assignments, in new squads, with new partners. It was not uncommon for those who worked in and around the vice squad to want to move elsewhere, as it was not widely considered a choice assignment, compared to homicide or armed robbery detectives, or better paying administrative positions in the department. Even the most resolute cop could get exhausted after a time dealing with one too many cases involving sex work, pornography, gambling, or drugs and alcohol. A homicide detective could potentially help put a murderer in jail but for cops working in vice, the sense of occupational achievement—a job well done—wasn't always as tangible. Sex workers, pimps, drug dealers, and loan sharks often returned to the same streets they'd been arrested on, occasionally before vice squad members had even finished filing their reports.

A cynic, or a conspiracy theorist, might suggest that it's curious that just as Bader and Robson were closing in on the street hustler investigation, these two officers with that much experience were moved off the case. But it would not be the only time the investigation seemed to be hampered—whether deliberately or not—by administrative manoeuvres and changes in course of action.

Bader remained with the crime prevention unit with new assignments and different partners, before eventually being moved to the Emergency Response Team, and later becoming a supervisor at a VPD firearms training facility. But while Robson was moving on, Bader hadn't yet seen the last of the Harris investigation.

Although progress on Bader and Robson's investigation had been paused, the VPD remained engaged with the wider issue of sex work in Vancouver. In September 1977, the department announced a new special squad to address the rising number of sex workers in the streets of downtown.

Dr John Lowman, a criminologist at Simon Fraser University who has studied sex work in multiple Canadian cities, notes that the vice squad task force's approach to street sex work largely backfired. "The police task forces moved sex workers off Davie Street into the adjoining side streets, reasoning that street prostitution would be less visible this way," Lowman says. "As a result, to people living in those side streets it must have seemed like prostitution was expanding, when, in fact, it was primarily being displaced."

City forms special squad to fight prostitution rise

The Vancouver police board agreed Wednesday to a special vice squad to crack down on street prostitution after police told the board a survey found more than 700 prostitutes — including at least 61 juvenile males — working the downtown area.

Police estimates placed the total annual income of the prostitutes, male and female, at more than $30 million.

Reacting to the police survey, the board also supported all police recommendations for legislative and policy changes to combat prostitution and agreed to forward the proposals to senior governments.

The recommendations and the figures were contained in a report police prepared specially for the board after recent controversy about the incidence of prostitution in Vancouver.

The report will be forwarded to B.C. Attorney-General Garde Gardom, federal Justice Minister Ron Basford, the B.C. Law Reform Commission and Vancouver city council.

The special anti-prostitution squad, which police said will be implemented immediately, will employ undercover officers to obtain evidence against both the prostitute and the client.

In their recommendations, which the board supported, police called on the Liquor Administration Board and the city licensing department to apply pressure to establishments catering to prostitutes and pimps.

They want the city to develop a plan to upgrade areas of Granville Street frequented by prostitutes.

And they want the Criminal Code amended to include a section pertaining to the

"Police" page 2

In September 1977, the VPD formed a new special vice squad to "crack down on street prostitution" after a survey found that more than 700 sex workers, including at least 61 juvenile males, were operating in downtown Vancouver.

The laws regarding sex work were greatly affected on a federal level by events in early 1978, with a landmark Supreme Court of Canada decision that had its genesis in an incident that occurred in 1975 on a street in downtown Vancouver. On May 8, twenty-year-old Debra Hutt was standing at Granville and Helmcken around 9:30 p.m. when she saw a car slowly approach the curb. Inside was a slim, soft-spoken, genial man named George Barclay. She smiled, and he returned the smile. Hutt got into the car.

"Hi," she said.

"Hi," Barclay said.

"Do you want a girl?" she asked him.

"What do you mean?"

"Do you want to go out?"

"Okay," he said.

"It's thirty dollars," she said.

"Oh, gosh, what will we do?" he asked.

"I'm a working girl," she said.

"Oh, what's that?" Barclay asked innocently.

"Do you want a girl?" she repeated.

"Okay, yes," he said.

"I'm a working girl. I'm a prostitute," Hutt said.

"Oh, I've never done this before," he said, almost overplaying the wide-eyed innocence.

"Oh."

"I'm staying at the Dufferin," he said, referring to a hotel a few blocks north at Seymour and Smithe. In the mid-1950s, the Dufferin was a modern upmarket hotel, but by 1975, the hotel was showing its age and catering to a less upscale crowd.

"Okay," she said.

"Will you do oral sex?" he asked.

"You mean a French?"

"Yeah."

"Oh, yes," she said.

"Okay," Barclay said.

"Let's go."[17]

Barclay, who was wearing a wire, drove to the rear of the Dufferin Hotel where he produced his badge, told Hutt he was an undercover police officer, and arrested her under section 195.1 of the Canadian Criminal Code, which stated, "Every person who solicits any person in a public place for the purposes of prostitution is guilty of an offence punishable on summary conviction."

Hutt was subsequently convicted, but through her Vancouver lawyer, Tony Serka, she fought the case all the way to the Supreme Court of Canada, whereby the court made a dramatic precedent-setting interpretation that quashed Hutt's conviction.

Previous solicitation laws had been difficult to enforce because the definition of soliciting itself was unclear. Sex work was not illegal, but the solicitation of it in a public place was. And just what constituted a *public* place was open to interpretation. The February 1978 Supreme Court ruling mandated that the soliciting had to be "pressing and persistent" in order for it to be illegal, and that a car was not a public place. Unless a sex worker was seen to be a nuisance, then police had no case. While the ruling in the Hutt case affected law enforcement policy nationwide, in Vancouver an additional bomb was dropped on the vice squad.

---

[17] Transcript from the Supreme Court of Canada, *Hutt v. the Queen*, [1978] 2 S.C.R. 476, decisions.scc-csc.ca/scc-csc/scc-csc/en/item/6076/index.do.

In December 1977, the appellate court case against the Penthouse Nightclub that had resulted in charges against the Filippone brothers resulted in a verdict of not guilty. Vice squad officers who had led the initial investigation, and Crown lawyers who had prosecuted the case to the tune of $2 million, were left devastated. Many of them felt that if the Penthouse couldn't be charged and convicted of profiting from prostitution, who in Vancouver could?

As a result of the Hutt decision, many arrests related to sex work that emerged from Mayor Volrich's street-sweeping campaign were thrown out. And with police unsure of what exactly "pressing and persistent" meant, combined with the result of the Penthouse case, the VPD effectively stopped charging street sex workers with solicitation. In November and December 1977 alone, there were 205 solicitation charges filed. In all of 1978, a mere 68 solicitation charges were filed. Now that the prevailing opinion among law enforcement was that arrests linked to prostitution would only lead to dismissals or petty fines, sex work—particularly in the West End—spread and expanded in the following years.

Even Serka, Hutt's lawyer, had strong words for the police. "The Hutt case was important because it defined soliciting, not because it opened the floodgates," he said. "The vice squad is sitting on its hands saying, 'We can't do anything. Change the law.' In fact, they are not enforcing the law. The people of the West End are right to say they have been shortchanged by enforcement. The vice squad is an embarrassment to the police department, as well as themselves."[18]

Although law enforcement regarding sex work in Vancouver became a murky affair, the situation with Wayne Harris and his co-defendants remained clear. The case went to trial in September 1978.

"That case got a lot of attention in town and around the courts," recalls retired judge Thomas Gove, who was a lawyer in private practice before being appointed to the BC provincial court. "It was partly because of some of the gossip and details of the whole case that was coming out, but it was also just who was involved. The Crown counsel was Jessie MacNeil—who could be particularly feisty in court."

Jessie MacNeil, like Wayne Harris, hailed from Nova Scotia. She had made a name for herself prosecuting some high-profile rape, assault, and kidnapping cases that had come before the courts in Vancouver. In her blistering final arguments in the Harris case she called him one of the most despicable human beings she'd

18 Glenn Bohn, "Men of the Vice Squad Ride by Night, Armed with Bylaw," *Vancouver Sun*, April 29, 1982, A9.

A member of the VPD vice squad detains a
West End sex worker, circa 1978.

ever dealt with, who as a pimp "had used Joanne, also known as Helga Harris,
to support his little forays with young men and drugs."

Although evidence suggested that Harris had helped Helga overcome heroin
addiction, Judge Douglas Wetmore commented in his sentencing that removing
someone from the slavery of addiction, and then subjecting her to another form of
enslavement was even worse. Wetmore called Harris a selfish and heartless person,
whose "own greed, desire, and pleasures surmounted any decency with respect
to other people. You quite clearly treated her as a slave and lived off her avails."[19]

Wetmore imposed a three-year jail term on Harris for living off the avails
of prostitution, keeping a common bawdy house, and gross indecency. But the
charges of contributing to juvenile delinquency were stayed.

Despite being considered a victim of Wayne Harris, Helga Harris was convicted
of keeping a common bawdy house in their Kitsilano apartment. Harris's associate

[19] "Judge Warns Prostitutes, Procurers to Stay Away from Residential Areas," *Vancouver Sun*,
September 30, 1978, 11.

Roger Longtin, now nineteen, with no previous criminal record, was given an eighteen-month suspended sentence and a $100 fine.

"I would be blind if I was unaware of the problem created in the West End," Wetmore said. "I can't help social planners there, but I can discourage bawdy houses in other areas."

This trial was significant not only because it resulted in Harris's conviction but also because of what *wasn't* addressed during the proceedings. There were no charges against Hal Keller, or any of those who had hired Harris. Keller wasn't even mentioned. It seems there wasn't enough evidence to go after those who had paid Harris for the services. Knowing what Keller and the others had been up to with Harris and proving it in court were worlds apart.

Meanwhile, vice squad detective Jim Maitland says that the police department had certainly not forgotten about Keller. Indeed, a second investigation would soon focus on Keller and others. But the vice squad had suddenly turned their attention toward a new target: Wendy King—and one of her noteworthy clients.

King's tenth-floor West End apartment at 945 Jervis Street had been under police surveillance during spring 1978 in what had initially been a narcotics investigation—not of King herself but King's live-in lover, Raymond Young, a suspected drug trafficker. The CLEU (Coordinated Law Enforcement Unit) did a wiretap on the apartment telephone, recording more than 300 conversations, two of which were with the chief justice of the BC Supreme Court, Judge John Farris, who had called to make dates to see King. Comparing this to her other phone calls, police determined that King was doing sex work out of her home. Additionally, CLEU investigators had photographed Farris coming from and going to King's apartment. Police eventually raided the apartment that November. No narcotics were found related to the Raymond Young case, but they did find King's coded address book of contacts, which contained 800 names—most of them clients—that included prominent people in Vancouver society and politics. Judge Farris resigned from the Supreme Court when his name was leaked and he learned the Canadian Judicial Council was investigating his conduct. But the names hidden in King's "trick book" captivated local media attention for months into the new year.

King pleaded guilty and was fined and sentenced to hours of community service, eventually telling her story in a ghostwritten memoir. Despite not naming names in the book, she was sued for libel by another judge whose thinly veiled pseudonym established that he too was one of King's clients, but unlike with Farris, he had never met her.

King worked from her apartment, or occasionally as an escort accompanying clients to restaurants and nightclubs; nevertheless, this scandal heightened public attention on the growing number of sex workers on the streets in Vancouver, particularly in the West End. Clamping down on apartments used as "bawdy houses" only pushed women to work on the potentially more dangerous streets. Furthermore, some in the media asked why King was punished and not her prominent customer. Judge Farris had resigned and returned to work as a lawyer in private practice, without ever having admitted he'd even so much as met Wendy King.

Wayne Harris spent a year in prison before being released on parole on October 2, 1979. We cannot know what convinced parole authorities that Harris, only a third of the way into his sentence, was ready for release. Harris's parole records and prison reports have long been expunged from the archives of Corrections Canada and the Parole Board of Canada. Rumours circulated that Harris had begun a sexual relationship with his parole officer. Police considered this to be just another example of how Harris could continually charm, con, and manipulate to get what he wanted. Based on the memories of police investigators and their notes from the period, and eventually on the media reports filed in the following months, Harris had convinced others he was a reformed man. But as soon as he hit the streets, he picked up where he left off. According to Detective Jim Maitland, he rejoined Helga and his old associate Ray Paris in seeking out street kids to introduce to his wealthy clientele, in particular one of his old contacts: U-Frame-It owner Hal Keller. As Keller's business prospered, his private parties grew.

And Harris's role expanded. He was no longer paid occasionally for his services—he now had a full-time position. Keller put Harris on a monthly company salary in an official capacity as a "bodyguard," but a more accurate job description would be that he brought people to Keller, instead of keeping them away. Harris wasn't the only new addition to the payroll. Many of the teenage boys Harris brought in were given positions in various stores of Keller's business. Some friends said Keller wanted to help the teenagers find stable employment, but others said it was his way of keeping the boys close to him.

But Keller's personal life only seemed to deteriorate. A friend later described the thirty-nine-year-old Keller leading the "sad life of a chickenhawk," seeking affection from one teenager after another who was attracted to him only for his wealth.[20] As the age group he sought got younger, the Vancouver police interest increased.

Harris may have thought he was better at covering his tracks now that he was back on the street. He had indeed become more discreet in the use of his telephone. But it was during a new police wiretap investigation focused on Keller's home that Harris's name resurfaced. These new wiretaps revealed multiple coded calls to Harris, and other activity that police suspected involved drug deals, as activities involving minors. Search warrants were obtained.

At 12:45 p.m. on November 30, 1979, investigators from the CLEU, the RCMP, and the VPD descended upon three locations at once: the homes of Keller in Point Grey and Harris in Kitsilano, and the head office of U-Frame-It at 1754 West 5th Avenue. Detective Jim Maitland once again monitored the case, along with Gord Bader, who was promoted out of the crime prevention unit and into the CLEU.

"I was there with a horseman [RCMP officer] named Lloyd Plante from Burnaby General Investigation Section and another muni [municipal VPD] named Murray Scott at Keller's office," recalls Bader. "Keller himself seemed okay—he was nervous as hell, but anybody can get nervous when police are searching your place."

Bader refrained from asking any probing questions about Keller's activities with Harris, his hustlers, and the parties involving minors. Keller was cordial but not overly cooperative as police searched the premises, with some employees mystified by the police presence. "At one point Keller left his office to go out to the main room while we were looking around. There was a painting on the wall, and I thought I'd look behind to see if there was a wall safe—there wasn't. But directly behind the frame of the painting I found a gun, a semi-auto .32 calibre handgun." Bader found it was loaded and placed it back behind the frame.

"What we really wanted from Keller was to eventually corner in on him a bit, tell him what we had, and get him to reveal names—get him to testify against others involved in the Harris ring," Bader says. "We knew so many other people were involved. While we knew he was guilty, he might be more be useful in helping take down the whole thing. I thought I'd ignore the gun for the time being and maybe press him about it later."

Bader spoke with an eighteen-year-old employee of U-Frame-It who acknowledged Keller's connections with Harris. He agreed to work confidentially with Bader and the police and revealed details of the underage sex work scene. Bader suspected that the employee was also involved.

[20] Ros Oberlyn, "'Sad Life' of a Chickenhawk," *Vancouver Sun*, July 7, 1980, 10.

Police expected to at least find some drugs or other incriminating evidence in the homes of Keller and Harris, but none was found.

In the following weeks, rumours about the police search circulated among friends and employees at U-Frame-It. Friends would later say that Keller was almost cavalier about the search, boldly asserting he had nothing to hide, and even stating that he felt the search of both his home and business was a form of police harassment. He felt he'd been targeted and vowed to fight any charges in court.

Others said that, privately, Keller was deeply worried. He feared the impact gross indecency charges and public exposure might have on him personally and on his business. His personal life was in tatters, and he believed that some of his employees were stealing from him. But most of all, Keller was worried about Wayne Harris.

Harris had first appeared in Keller's life two years earlier as a friend. Harris was charming and Keller found his roguishness appealing. Keller felt that Harris could be trusted. When Harris was convicted as a pimp, it would have been easy for him to rat on Keller. But Harris kept quiet and never named him in the trial. Hiring Harris again after his brief stint in jail was like a gesture of appreciation for his silence. But Harris had become a dangerous figure to be around.

Keller became increasingly worried that Harris would blackmail him. After all, he knew the times and places that Keller had engaged in sex with boys. He knew the names of the boys. Perhaps Harris's efforts to befriend Keller were all an attempt to place himself deep enough in Keller's world to exploit what he knew? Perhaps Harris wouldn't even appear responsible for the blackmail but use someone he knew or hired to do the task? Everyone who dealt with Harris kept saying that he only looked out for himself. Harris adamantly said that he had no appetite to go back to prison to finish his sentence or to be prosecuted for any new crimes. Keller worried that if he attempted to cut a deal with police, or become an informant, there was no telling what Harris would do to protect himself.

Since the police raid, Keller's conversations with Harris had been cold, barely cordial. They'd both put on a front, pretending to laugh off the search. Police hadn't found anything, but for Keller, this was new territory. Harris had come from the streets and knew how to endure police questioning. Keller was not a man used to this kind of pressure. Did both men now think the other had tried to gain the advantage and escape prosecution by ratting out the other?

Keller had scheduled a vacation for New Year's Eve with a plan to travel to Hawaii with his fourteen-year-old lover. The boy was a ward of the BC superintendent of child welfare. He was staying with Keller at his Point Grey home with the knowledge of the human resources ministry, which was considering Keller's application to become the boy's legal guardian. The teen's social worker, unaware that Keller had come under police investigation, had approved the trip to Hawaii.

The trip had been planned before the police raid. And now more than ever perhaps it was considered to be a welcome getaway. Keller could take his mind off things, get out of the winter rain, and relax on the beach far away from his concerns, from police search warrants, and from Wayne Harris.

On Boxing Day, Keller went to his office, ostensibly to catch up on some paperwork, to clear his desk before the vacation. He worked late into the night and didn't return home, which wasn't out of character. He worked hard at his business. And 1979 had been a pivotal year for the company. It had undergone such incredible growth in seven years. Now was a good time for some year-end stock-taking—what was the future of U-Frame-It? Where was it headed? Some had suggested that Keller sell the entire business off to investors and take an early retirement. But there was also so much more room to expand the operation. He was only thirty-nine, and he had many good years to work ahead of him if he wished.

All of these opportunities and potential life choices became irrelevant, though, because the following morning, word had reached police—Hal Keller was dead.

CHAPTER 9

The Fix

At eight a.m. on Thursday, December 27, 1979, twenty-one-year-old U-Frame-It employee Ross Murray arrived at the company's main office to open for the day. The building, which still exists today, was a warehouse and office space that not only stored company materials but also held the administrative desks several of the company's management personnel. Murray figured he was the first to arrive that day. He had begun browsing some mail at his desk when another junior employee, Daniel Daigle, arrived minutes after him.

When the two men noticed that Keller's office light was on, they wondered if their boss was already at work. Murray called out to Keller and got no response. His office was empty. Both Murray and Daigle then walked down to the building's interior parking bay, where they found their boss's car—the familiar brown four-door Mercury Zephyr sedan—parked in its usual space.

As they approached the car, they noticed Keller in the driver's seat. A vacuum hose had been connected to the car's exhaust and stretched into the rear window of the vehicle. They saw the keys in the ignition, but the car's engine was off. On the passenger seat beside him, a sweater of Keller's was neatly folded.

The two men shouted at Keller, opening the door to see if he was alive. But they soon realized he was dead. Looking down at the car mats, they noticed that, curiously, Keller's shoes were untied and his laces stretched open.

Frantic, they darted back into the office to call the police. The first constables to arrive secured the scene and performed cursory interviews of the employees.

News of Keller's death quickly circulated among police investigators at both the CLEU (Coordinated Law Enforcement Unit) and the city vice squad, who had been monitoring Keller for many weeks. The news spread outside of police circles, too. At ten a.m., Harris and Helga came to the U-Frame-It office. When questioned, Harris only said he was a friend of Keller's and had learned of his death from mutual acquaintances. Harris was not the only friend or associate of Keller's who arrived that morning, but the CLEU and vice squad officers who knew Harris well feared that the homicide officers who weren't up to speed on the Harris-Keller investigation would not ask Harris the right questions—or enough of them.

Detective Mike Barnard of the Major Crime Section led the investigation. But Jim Maitland would eventually go on record, listing his concerns in a memo that today remains in the VPD file on the death of Hal Keller.

There were a few puzzling aspects to the scene in Keller's car. No fingerprints were found on the vacuum hose that had been connected to the exhaust. Had another party staged the scene and wiped it? Keller's keys were found in the ignition, but the engine was off and the gas tank was nearly full. Who turned it off? And there was the odd situation with Keller's shoes—they were on, but the laces were undone and completely loosened. Had his shoes been slipped on after he'd been dragged from somewhere else and placed in the car?

Police also considered the scene might not be as suspicious as it immediately seemed. People who committed suicide using exhaust fumes tended to lie in the back seat of a car more often than sit in the front seat—but it did happen sometimes. And there were instances where those who sat in the driver's seat loosened their shoes or took them off to get comfortable. It was also not uncommon for a would-be suicide victim to have second thoughts, and then turn off the ignition but be unable to extricate themselves from the vehicle in their stupor from the fumes. This could have been the scenario that left a full tank in Harris's car.

Typically, it takes just five short minutes to breathe in enough carbon monoxide to kill an adult. If Keller's death was set up to look like a suicide, he surely would not have gone along without a fight. If he had been drugged, or was already dead and then placed in the car, it probably would have taken two men to move Keller's 190 pounds of dead weight. But there were no scratches on him or other signs that he'd been in an altercation. His clothing was not rumpled or ripped. No barbiturates or alcohol were found in Keller's system during the autopsy, so it didn't appear that he was drunk or had been drugged prior to his death. The official cause of death was listed as carbon monoxide poisoning.

Suspicious details of the scene of death aside, it was the circumstances of Keller's personal life that turned investigators in another direction. Detective Barnard learned that Keller had a gotten into a fight with his teenage lover at Keller's home. Keller probably anticipated that a police investigation was closing in on him. He would have known that such publicity would have disastrous effects on his business, his personal reputation, and his application to become the legal guardian of the teenage boy. However, although major crimes investigators were made aware of the extent of Keller's dealings with Harris, they believed Harris was not a suspect. And there weren't any other apparent viable suspects who might have wanted Keller dead. In the end, his death was deemed a suicide.

Gord Bader was on holiday when the news reached him that Keller was dead. He was troubled to hear of the Major Crime Section's ruling. Days earlier Bader had spoken with Keller, who, though nervous, didn't seem despondent. Bader was told that Keller's autopsy had uncovered nothing suspicious, but his gut instinct told him something else was going on.

He contacted Barnard and told him it would be worthwhile to check for needle marks, in case Keller had been drugged. Barnard told him that none had been found, and there hadn't been any other evidence to conclude that Keller was murdered. And, besides, by that point, the body had already been buried.

"The standard toxicology reports they did back then were basic and didn't include refined searches unless there was a reason for it," says Bader. "Advanced autopsies aren't done on every dead body that lands in the morgue, and if something in the end looks like a suicide, it's just simply ruled to be that—and that's the end of it. But I always thought a refined toxicology report should have been done, to see what might have been revealed, and it might have answered some lingering questions a few of us still had."

Hal Keller had planned to ring in the new decade in Hawaii with friends; instead, a private funeral service was held for him the morning of December 31, 1979, in Mountain View Cemetery.

The Keller file, Case #79-66689, though ruled a suicide, was classified as open by the Vancouver Police Department. It remains open partly because of concerns listed by Detective Jim Maitland, which suggested that if additional evidence came to light, there might be a way to finally conclude the case. It has remained open for more than forty years.

Like when Bader and Robson were reassigned in 1977, the death of Hal Keller in 1979 once again slowed any further investigation into the other members of the Harris ring. Other persons of interest in this case who were connected to Harris—and there were many—seemingly receded from the police's immediate concern. Did Keller's death end any further initiative by the VPD to investigate Harris? If Keller's death had been ruled a homicide, would it have triggered a deeper investigation? One that would have exposed connections between Keller and Harris that were already known in vice squad circles? At least one former VPD detective thinks so.

Gord Bader is still vexed when he recalls the Harris-Keller investigation. Aside from Maitland, Bader had surveilled Hal Keller more than any other officer. "To this day, I still think Keller was murdered," Bader says. "There were some outstanding leads. We had Harris on a wiretap conversation saying to somebody that he had been first to find the body—but he didn't want to have anything to do with it. We never did find out more. People moved on to other things after Keller died. I don't know in the end if Harris was involved. Or if Harris had got somebody else to do it. But it just felt too convenient that Keller died right then, and I wish it would have been looked into further. Maybe a lot more would have been exposed."

Vancouver police were unable to definitively fill the gap and connect Hal Keller's death to the world of Wayne Harris. In July 1980, that void was suddenly and surprisingly filled by the last person anyone would have expected—Wayne Harris himself.

In early 1980, Harris had violated his parole when he was found in possession of stolen property and was pulled over for driving while impaired, but the charges were stayed or dismissed. However, after a physical altercation with a police officer at a Davie Street restaurant in June, Harris was sent back to prison. While serving his sentence, he was interviewed by *Vancouver Sun* reporter Ros Oberlyn.

Oberlyn wrote an article for the July 7, 1980, issue of the paper called "'Sad Life' of a Chickenhawk," which was part of a four-part series on the Davie Street sex trade.[21] She changed the names of those involved but, based on the timeline and the characters presented, it is obvious that the story is about Keller, Harris, and Harris's old associate Ray Paris.

Oberlyn tells the story of a "monied businessman in his late 30s mixed up in the Davie Street scene last year." And she mentions "two men whose names are repeatedly linked with juvenile prostitution" and who profited from it. The businessman she describes lived in an expensive home in a fashionable neighbourhood and owned half a dozen outlets across the country. He's then described as committing suicide just before a planned trip to Hawaii "with his lover ... a 14-year-old boy." This businessman also had on payroll a man, named Frank in

21 Ros Oberlyn, "'Sad Life' of a Chickenhawk," *Vancouver Sun*, July 7, 1980, 10.

the article, whom police were investigating for alleged connections with drugs, stolen property, and prostitution. The article states that "Frank" had first been sentenced in September 1978 (the date of Harris's sentencing), after being convicted of living off the avails of prostitution with his wife. He is described as having returned to prison after a parole violation, with other details that match Harris's criminal record.

The article mentions that a report by a group called Taking Responsible Action for Children and Youth identified "Frank" as a well-known pimp and ringleader of juvenile sex work. The article detailed how he recruited boys and girls: "One was a 15-year-old runway girl spotted on the street by Frank's wife. The other was a boy, also 15 and a runaway, who was picked up hitchhiking by one of Frank's associates. In both cases, the teenagers were treated to a meal and offered a place to stay." At the apartment, runaways were given drugs and forced into sexual activities with adults. "Later they were introduced to other adults who wanted to have sex with juveniles."

According to Oberlyn, Frank "does not match the old-fashioned stereotype of a pimp—the sly character in flashy dress who stands on a street corner drumming up business for a stable of prostitutes. He is a likeable person with an engaging manner." Frank denied that he had ever been a pimp for anyone but his wife and further claimed that he had never coaxed teenagers into sex work or earned any money from it. He also denied that he dealt in drugs or stolen property. But Frank admitted that he liked to have sex with boys and had introduced several boys to businessmen for sex. He also admitted to having his wife lure boys back to their home but said he had quit doing that.

Frank acted like he had been providing a public service. "The kid's going to hustle anyway," "Frank" told the *Vancouver Sun*. "Now, which is better, for him to stand on the street or for him to stay off the street and let me introduce him to someone who is going to at least be half decent to him? Then he won't get stabbed or beat up, or forced to do something."

When asked how dangerous it was on the street for a young person, "Frank" waved his arm in the direction of the prison cells. "It's like putting a 12 year old kid in here," he said. "When I see a kid, 12, 13, or 14 or 15 standing on the street corner in the rain and going out and having sex with some of these men who are so filthy it's unreal. I think it's disgusting, because—it was for me."

"Frank" explained that he knew first-hand what could happen to a boy on the street because he was hustling at the age of twelve, after a childhood

Photo by Steve Bosch (Vancouver Sun Archives)

Two young sex workers on the streets of the West End, July 1979.

spent in twenty-two different foster homes. When he first started, he hated the men who used him sexually and despised what he was doing. But he didn't see himself, now, as an exploiter of children. Instead, he seemed to consider himself a noble character who could help these kids with a place to stay or a train ticket home.

Oberlyn observed that these runaway teenagers on Davie Street revered "Frank." "They look up to him. They talk about how he is working toward a black belt in the martial arts. 'They get a vicarious rush [from him],' said one source. 'He is the epitome of what they, themselves, think is romantic ... an overall, consummate hustler."

Oberlyn asked "Frank" why he thought young people were drawn to him. His answer went against the grain of what just about everyone who had ever met him had said—that he was only interested in himself.

A VPD vice squad officer on stakeout surveils West Georgia Street from a window in the Hotel Vancouver, 1982.

Photo by Mark van Manen (Vancouver Sun Archives)

"Affection," he said plainly. "Somebody who cares a little bit. Somebody who will talk to him and listen to his complaints."

By 1980, the VPD's general vice squad was focusing most of its energy and resources onto a single target—one that was increasingly difficult to manage. The division that addressed gambling was winnowed down to just two detectives. And since Mayor Volrich's initial declaration of war on obscenity, vice had gone four years without a serious complaint about pornography. More and more, it seemed that vice's main priority was to control Vancouver's sex trade.

A police crackdown near the intersection of Georgia and Hornby Streets had cleared sex workers out of the area by the end of 1979. And under a new directive, the VPD had mobilized about thirty uniformed officers to carry out regular nighttime patrols of the West End. But even that initiative had unintended consequences, as a greater police presence at night pushed sex workers to take to the streets earlier in day.

"Ladies of the Evening Forced to Work the Afternoon Shift," read the July 9, 1979, headline in the *Vancouver Sun*. The accompanying article said sex workers complained that police regularly "harassed 'working girls' by driving up while they are talking to a client, which usually results in the client walking away and the girl losing out."[22]

Both Mike Harcourt, who had become Vancouver's mayor in 1980, and Chief Constable Bob Stewart had been asking the federal government to pass stronger laws regulating sex work. And arresting people in undercover operations didn't seem like it was yielding the desired results. The VPD needed a new approach. In 1980, only 2 of the VPD's 131 detectives were female, neither of whom were on the vice squad. But in April of that year, the department enlisted two female constables to put on fur coats and high leather boots to pose as sex workers. The aim was to enforce a new bylaw that authorized fines from $250 to $2,000 for anyone caught selling or buying sexual services on city streets. The results of their first night out, though, were lacklustre. For their entire shift the two managed to lure only four male customers, one of whom was carrying 4,000 pennies.

Around five a.m. on October 2, 1980, nineteen-year-old John Joseph Ogden climbed a twenty-metre (sixty-foot) tree near the bandstand in Alexandra Park, across the street from English Bay. Considering that he had consumed a large amount of alcohol and taken methamphetamines the night before, it's a miracle that he didn't fall from the branches and seriously injure himself. It was even more startling that he had climbed the tree carrying a .22 calibre rifle.

Nestled in the branches, Ogden aimed the rifle at a street lamp on Davie two blocks away and fired. He shifted his aim to a street sign and fired. As Ogden took potshots at other random targets in the area, the sound of gunshots echoed through the early-morning air and toward the apartment blocks along Beach Avenue.

The first person hit was thirty-eight-year-old Frederick Simpson, who had left his nearby Haro Street apartment for a walk along the seawall. He had even

---

[22] Larry Pynn, "Ladies of the Evening Forced to Work the Afternoon Shift," *Vancouver Sun*, July 9, 1979, 12.

Photo by Brian Kent (Vancouver Sun Archives)

Vancouver police, including Corporal George Kristensen (centre), close in on a West End sniper who fired on targets around Davie and Denman Streets and injured three, including one police officer, on October 2, 1980.

greeted Ogden when he'd passed him on the sidewalk minutes earlier. Simpson heard the shot and felt the bullet graze his arm. Unable to determine where the shot had come from, Simpson ran and later drove himself to Vancouver General Hospital, where he was treated and later released. Another man driving down Beach Avenue was nicked by flying glass from a shot that came through his windshield.

By 5:30 a.m., multiple reports of shots fired near the English Bay bathhouse were called in to Vancouver police. Practically every available officer on duty that morning in District One poured onto the scene, triangulated the shots, and cordoned off a six-block square section of apartment buildings. By morning rush hour, police were rerouting buses and turning cars away from the area as the bullets continued to fly.

Thirty-six-year-old Vancouver police corporal Grant Driver was shot in the right forearm as he stood in front of the bathhouse and was immediately taken to hospital for treatment. An RCMP helicopter joined the search for the shooter, but Ogden continued to fire away unseen, hidden by the canopy of tall trees.

Ogden had fired close to thirty rounds by the time he climbed down and fled the scene. Witnesses followed his movements and just after eight a.m., a tactical squad with guns drawn, supported by the canine unit, cornered him in the alleyway of the 1500 block of Davie Street. Police apprehended Ogden hidden behind a parked station wagon. More than an hour later, police found the rifle and seventy-nine live cartridges in the tree that Ogden had perched in. By lunch, the area was secured.

Thankfully, no one was killed. Corporal Driver eventually returned to duty.

In February 1981, Ogden was put on trial. Defence lawyer Jim Thompson claimed that society was to blame for Ogden's violent outburst for "permitting the Granville Street lifestyle and Davie Street lifestyle." Odgen was convicted of attempted murder and sent to prison for five years.

This was not the first open shooting incident in the West End. A sniper, believed to be hiding in the 1100 block of Jervis Street, randomly fired several rounds on Davie Street in June 1973. The shooter was never caught. But the 1980 incident in particular fuelled the notion that the West End was becoming an increasingly dangerous, unlivable neighbourhood. Sex workers walking along the sidewalks was one thing; being shot at was another thing entirely.

Vancouver's West End had even begun attracting negative media attention outside the city. In October 1981, the *Calgary Herald* featured an exposé headlined "Sexual Supermarket" that described the scene outside of St. Paul's Anglican Church on Jervis Street, where sex workers occasionally gathered during church services and funerals: "A young blonde woman talks to the middle-aged driver and then climbs in, as two male homosexual prostitutes chat on church steps waiting for business ... Walk another block and you're in the territory of the transvestites, men who dress as women, and transsexuals, males who have undergone sex change operations or exhibit features of both sexes." The article went on to describe a nine-year-old boy playing in the area who "was propositioned by an adult male, only to be chased by an angry male hooker who thought the boy was stealing his 'trick,' as customers are called."[23]

While out-of-town journalists may have depicted the West End scene as menacing and out of control, some locals took it all in stride. "You saw the hookers and working girls on the way to school," recalls Doug Sarti, who grew up in the West End, and was thirteen years old in 1980. He's the son of *Vancouver Sun* columnist Bob Sarti and the co-author of *The Georgia Straight: A 50th Anniversary Celebration*. "I'd see them when I walked up to Davie Street on my own when I was a kid, but I never feared them. Sometimes they'd call out to you, 'Hey sweetie,' but they never really bothered us and we never really bothered them."

---

[23] George Oake, "Sexual Supermarket—West End Vancouver's Bizarre Business Has Residents Fuming," *Calgary Herald*, October 30, 1981, 86.

Doug says, "it was a colourful neighbourhood to grow up in while all that was happening. But as much as there was so much news going on about the West End—the concerns, or the fear—it always seemed to be coming from outside the West End rather from people in it—or at least as kids it was just normal to us to see condoms in the alleyways or people having sex outside somewhere."

If there were mixed results eliminating the sex trade with increased patrols and a greater uniformed police presence in the West End, the city's next move was to try to interrupt the traffic toward sex workers altogether.

On the afternoon of November 16, 1981, City of Vancouver workers began installing concrete barriers and A-frame traffic barricades held in place by lock and chain along a number of West End streets. Placed at intervals along the side streets, these traffic diverters were spread across an area bounded roughly by Bute Street to the west, Nelson Street to the north, Cardero Street to the east, and Burnaby Street to the south. City council announced the barriers would be put in place in "an attempt to deal with the prostitution/nuisance problems in the West End." The project would come at a cost of $28,000.

The diversions were not met with universal approval from residents. Local call-in radio shows and letter-to-the-editor newspaper sections were flooded with complaints. People were cut off from easy access to their own apartment buildings. Street parking was now blocked. One outraged letter to the *Vancouver Sun* asked if moats and drawbridges in the neighbourhood were next.

Firefighters from the No. 6 fire hall at 1001 Nicola Street, a fixture in the West End since 1907, expressed reservations as well. "We aim for a four-minute response time on emergency inhalator calls for heart attack victims and between two or three minutes on fires," said firefighter Andy McNaughton. He said that during one of their test runs, it took them seventy-five additional seconds to unlock the barricades and close them again. "If you add more than a minute to that, what are the chances you're going to have problems?"[24]

When asked about the traffic diversions by curious media, sex workers seemed to be more amused than anything else. The barricades set up to thwart their trade on side streets actually tended to help their business. "Oh, they're great; we love 'em," a sex worker told a reporter for the *Vancouver Sun*, noting that all drivers were now forced to slow down along traffic-controlled streets, which gave

[24] Robert Sarti, "Traffic Diverters Irk Firemen," *Vancouver Sun*, November 21, 1981, 1.

A reporter interviews a West End sex worker next to one of the "temporary" barricades placed in a number of city streets in November 1981.

sex workers a better opportunity to strike up a conversation with a potential customer. Once again, a project intended to curb sex work led to unintended consequences.

Although the traffic closures were branded as temporary at the time, they were soon replaced by more permanent structures. Within the next year, city engineers installed additional curbs to deny automobile access to many West End side streets, and created landscaped parklets to fill in closed-off streets.

The plan to divert traffic in the West End goes back as far as 1973, when the City of Vancouver established a West End planning centre, staffed by urban and social planning experts, as well as members of the engineering departments, with the goal to prepare an open space policy for the West End. Architects were commissioned to create traffic-calming projects west of Denman Street—small parklets designed to have "a casual air, almost undesigned, and feel as if they have always been part of the urban fabric." [25]

The "temporary" traffic diversions have remained in place for forty years, and as the trees in these spaces have grown and matured, the closures now seem permanent. Getting rid of them to open up West End traffic would be quite likely to summon a new group of residents wanting to keep them.

[25] Gordon Price, "Original Greening: How the West End Went from Pavement to Plaza," *Viewpoint Vancouver*, September 10, 2019, viewpointvancouver.ca/2019/09/10/original-greening-how-the-west-end-went-from-pavement-to-plaza/ (accessed August 11, 2021).

CHAPTER 10

A Bad Collar

When Wayne Harris was released again from prison in September 1981, he returned to a Vancouver and a West End that had changed so much since he'd left as the king of street hustlers when he was convicted in 1978.

With Hal Keller dead, Harris's largest benefactor was gone, and he was broke. Many of those who had met Harris through Keller now steered clear of him—perhaps figuring they might somehow suffer the same fate—or somehow be dragged down by the police scrutiny that never seemed far behind him. Either way, Harris's calls to old friends and associates went unreturned.

Those on the streets had also decided that Harris was too much of a heat score. Rumours circulated among many who'd dealt with Harris on theft jobs or drug deals that he'd become a police informant—and within the criminal fraternity of the Vancouver underworld, Harris become someone who was considered best to avoid. It turned out they had reason to be worried.

"Harris for years was a police informant," recalls Al Robson. "I remember one guy on the department dealt with him regularly. He wasn't so much an informant that one could always go to or [who] would freely offer tips up to police. He was in it for himself. So when it looked like he might get arrested or charged with something he was involved with, he'd rat on accomplices, like some of the kids who had stolen for him, just so he could avoid getting in trouble himself. I don't know if any of those kids he saw one day knew he was ratting on them the next."

The revelation that Harris was being investigated for serious crimes—while also providing police with information related to other criminal activities—put Harris and the VPD in a complicated ethical relationship. Had Harris ever avoided prosecution for crimes because of his role as an informant? Most vice squad members who interacted with Harris recall him being surly and uncooperative. Had Harris's slithery nature allowed him to give police investigators information regarding stolen property but steer them away from more serious inquiries that could have led to child exploitation charges? Most police who knew of Harris at that time deny that was a factor, because the criminal activities that he was involved in with drugs or stolen property were low level enough that they were treated separately—the ultimate goal was always to convict Harris as a pimp.

Either way, there was little room for a 1970s pimp in a 1980s world. Just a few years earlier, Harris had groomed teenagers from the street to hustle older men on his behalf or abused the teens himself. But now there were so many underage sex workers on West End streets, those clients didn't need Harris anymore. And the sex workers had no interest in sharing their pay with Harris when they could work the streets alone.

The West End continued to be a turbulent, notorious neighbourhood. By 1981, the sex trade there was developing into what *Maclean's* magazine would later describe as "a curbside brothel open from noon to 4 a.m., seven days a week."[26] Dissatisfied with the efforts of the VPD to address the issue, local residents' groups became more active and outspoken. That year a new West End community lobby group known as CROWE (Concerned Residents of the West End) began a steady campaign of petitions and reports. As historian Daniel Francis notes in his book *Red Light Neon*, the activists objected to "all the nuisance activities that accompanied [sex workers]: the noise, littering, intimidation and general crime that came with the transformation of the neighbourhood into an open-air sex bazaar."[27]

In 1984, a new group of protesters took an even more aggressive stance against sex workers on West End streets with a Shame the Johns campaign. The group held protests on the very sidewalks where the sex trade occurred, using humiliation as a tool to discourage clients from approaching workers. The protesters had been inspired by a *Vancouver Sun* article by columnist Rick Ouston, who had implored West End residents to address the increasing number of underage sex workers who were appearing on neighbourhood streets. These youth were abused not only by the pimps who controlled them but also by their clientele, suggested Ouston, so they needed protecting. The group held placards calling out the johns, photographed those who spoke to sex workers, and, most brazenly, took down licence plate numbers and, thanks to like-minded contacts within vehicle registration authorities and insurance companies, obtained the names

[26] Brian D. Johnson, "Selling Sex on the Street," *Maclean's*, April 16, 1984, 60b.
[27] Daniel Francis, *Red Light Neon: A History of Vancouver's Sex Trade* (Vancouver: Subway Books, 2006), 96.

Protest and counterprotest: West End sex workers and Shame the Johns campaigners square off in 1984. At centre (with white purse) is "Michelle," who was spotlighted in the documentary *Hookers on Davie*, released that same year.

and addresses of the drivers, threatening to publicly humiliate these customers. They even paid for a "Shame the Johns" billboard that stood tall on Davie Street.

These tactics led to hostile confrontations among pimps, sex workers, customers, and protesters, which created a menacing atmosphere along West End streets. Local news broadcasts depicted the neighbourhood as a kind of tawdry war zone. Whereas a documentary by filmmakers Janis Cole and Holly Dale called *Hookers on Davie* offered a deeper, more nuanced view of the situation from the perspectives of the sex workers. The release of the film brought national attention to the realities of the West End street sex trade, and it was one of the few mainstream depictions at the time that humanized the sex workers in this community.

Increasingly, there was no place for Wayne Harris in the rapidly changing West End community. Even his old associates had turned on him. He'd had a falling out with Ray Paris who, according to police sources, had taken over Harris's failing hustling operation after Harris had gone back to prison. Even Helga Harris had finally left him and returned to Manitoba.

"I remember Wayne was broke, going around to some of the old clubs looking to even borrow just a couple of dollars," says Faces nightclub worker Art Robinson. "He was down on his luck then and pretty desperate. It was pathetic."

The Shame the Johns campaign began in the West End in 1984.

In 1981, Harris began working as a doorman at Numbers, a Davie Street gay nightclub that had opened in 1980 and is still in operation today. He was certainly fit and strong enough to be a capable bouncer, though there were rarely any serious security issues at the club. But the job allowed him to continue his nickel-and-dime marijuana dealing to friends and regulars. Harris is remembered as well liked by his co-workers, though many may not have known the full extent of his criminal past. His three-year sentence served for being a pimp was not something to be shared in casual conversation.

The possibly more staid course of Harris's life came, literally, to a crashing halt in 1982. He was injured and hospitalized after his car was hit by a train. The exact details of the collision are difficult to ascertain. News archives appear to not have any reports on the accident. Freedom of Information requests and inquiries by the author with first responders, auto insurance, and rail company archives reveal little. Information on motor vehicle accidents and claims over forty years old are no longer kept.

All that remains are the memories of Harris's friends who recall how seriously he was injured. "Things really changed for him when he was hit. He was different after that," recalls a friend of Wayne and Helga's from the mid-1970s.

"I don't know what had happened exactly with the accident, if his car had stalled on the train track, or if he was trying to outrun the train—he always had souped-up muscle cars. But he was in the hospital for a while. The head injury he sustained was bad. He had to practically relearn how to talk. Wayne had always been very 'with it' and quick witted, but he just wasn't the same after the accident."

Andre Tardif, who had met Harris at the old Taurus bathhouse in the Bon Accord Hotel in the early 1970s, recalls seeing Harris sometime after his release from the hospital, at the Taurus once again. "We had sex there," Tardif confesses. "But he didn't move or talk. That was it. He was much different than when I had first met him."

After the accident, Harris submitted a personal injury claim, for which he was represented in court by lawyer Valmond Romilly, who later became a provincial court judge and has since retired. (When contacted by the author and asked about the case from forty years earlier, Romilly stated he could only vaguely remember representing Harris and recalled nothing further from the case.)

Harris thought his life had truly bottomed out with his accident. Some vice squad members who had investigated him said the accident was a brand of karmic justice that couldn't have happened to a more deserving person. But good fortune seems to spare a smile for both our angels and devils, and Harris was awarded a settlement by Canadian Pacific Railway that police believed to be between $50,000 and $100,000. A financial settlement that large, especially in the early 1980s, went a long way toward securing his future. Harris invested some of the money and still had plenty left over to buy a new car. Despite the accident, Harris still liked flashy cars, and he bought a Pontiac Firebird Trans Am, still the epitome of cool for many in the early '80s.

The financial settlement set Harris on a better course. Despite the trouble he'd been in over the years, and the severity of the accident, his future, oddly, looked better than perhaps any other time in his life.

Harris stopped working at Numbers after the accident but kept in touch with staff there. On April 30, 1984, he dropped into the bar for a drink and played pool with a man who appeared to be in his early twenties. The young man, though not as well known around town as Wayne, was recognized by a few other patrons as someone who'd been around the local gay bars and nightlife for a couple of years. It was an otherwise unremarkable quiet Monday night—except it would turn out to be the last night Wayne Harris was seen alive.

Two days later, on May 2, just before seven o'clock, police responded to a call that a body had been found in the trunk of a car, parked on the north side of Lost Lagoon in Stanley Park. Police checked the number on the plates over the radio and confirmed that the car, a Pontiac Firebird Trans Am, was owned by Wayne Harris.

Harris was, of course, known to police, even by Les Yeo—a District One constable just two years into his police career who attended the scene that day. Yeo had seen Harris around Davie Street, and senior officers in the vice squad had told him that, considering Harris's past, even if he seemed to be on the straight and narrow now, he was worth keeping an eye on.

"He had been beaten badly," recalls Yeo. "But the thing that stands out to me more than anything else is once we found him in the trunk, how difficult it was to get him out of there. If you know Trans Ams, the trunk inside is big enough, but the opening is a lot smaller. Rigor mortis had set in. Harris was a big guy, and it took several of us pulling on an arm here or a leg there to get him out. After him being dead for a while, that wasn't pleasant."

Harris had been left naked, wrapped in some bloodied blankets. It was clear he had suffered grave head injuries. After police took photographs of the scene, Harris's body was taken to the morgue for an autopsy, and the Trans Am was towed to the police impound lot.

The news about Wayne Harris's murder quickly spread among those who knew him in the West End scene. It came as a shock. Many had thought that if the word "murder" were ever attached to Wayne Harris, it would be because he was the assailant, not the victim. Had he finally ripped off the wrong person? Had someone targeted him for the windfall of settlement money he'd recently come into? Or did someone finally decide Wayne Harris knew too much and was better off dead? The homicide was of particular interest to many in the vice squad who knew all of Harris's trespasses. Gord Bader and Al Robson hoped the murder might reveal more than the investigation into Hal Keller had ever produced.

Photos by VPD forensic photographer, provided to author by investigator

On May 2, 1984, Police responded to a call that body had been found in the trunk of a car parked at North Lagoon Drive.

The investigation of Harris's murder moved quickly. The day after his body was found, Major Crime Section investigators went through photos and address books found in Harris's apartment, attempting to track his last few days and hours. The autopsy revealed some pills and alcohol in Harris's system. Helga Harris, his next of kin, was notified of the murder at her home in Winnipeg. Having left Harris two years earlier, she was never considered a suspect.

It didn't take long for police to show up at Harris's last known place of employment, Numbers. Two patrons who had been there the night Harris was last seen told investigators they saw him playing pool with a man in his early twenties named Neall Mayers, who was known to be a small-time drug dealer in the West End. Police discovered that Mayers had disappeared from Vancouver after that evening.

By May 5, 1984, the hunt was on, with Mayers now considered a person of interest in the case. His name was entered into the Canadian Police Information Centre (CPIC) computer system that would alert the VPD if Mayers was stopped by police anywhere else in the country. But Mayers was no longer in Canada. Major crimes investigators were later able to piece together that he simply walked across a relatively unmonitored area of the US–Canada border near Abbotsford, BC, and made his way to Sudden Valley, Washington, just outside of Bellingham. There he broke into the summer home of Vancouver physician Dr Carlos Guzman. There may have been a personal relationship between the two men, but there was most certainly a business one. Guzman was already the subject of a VPD narcotics squad investigation and later that month was

c/o Kevin Dale McKeown

Neall Mayers after his prison release, circa 1989.

arrested for cocaine trafficking. Guzman would also be fined by the College of Physicians and Surgeons of BC for improperly prescribing pills. Guzman appeared to be at least one of Mayers' drug sources.

Mayers then fled to his parents' home in San Bruno, California. The investigation later revealed he had confessed to the murder in a phone call to his parents from Dr Guzman's summer home. By May 15, Vancouver police learned he had made it to San Bruno. A warrant was issued, and Mayers was picked up by San Bruno police.

Shortly thereafter VPD staff sergeant Rich Rollins and VPD investigator Pat Harrison flew to San Francisco, where they were welcomed by US Marshals, who helped escort Mayers from San Bruno to the San Francisco airport.

"Mayers was fine coming back. There was no trouble," says Rollins, who was head of the Harris murder case. "We put the handcuffs on him in the front and draped a jacket over his handcuffs so it just looked like he was walking with a coat over his hands, and we just got on the plane before the rest of the passengers got on board." Mayers and the two plainclothes police officers just looked like three men on a business trip.

Rollins recalls that Mayers said nothing on the flight home, but once back in police custody in Vancouver, he was interrogated, and a vivid story of what happened the night Harris was killed unfolded. The details were revealed in an April 1986 second-degree murder trial, providing a glimpse into the private lives of both Wayne Harris and Hal Keller.

During the trial, Mayers stated he had met Harris at Numbers. He claimed he had previously known him only by reputation and, despite being leery of him, found the conversation they had over a game of pool enjoyable. After a couple of hours at the bar, Harris accepted Mayers's invitation to come back to his home at 950 Bidwell Street for some drinks and cocaine that Harris had purchased at the club. The two took Harris's car to the apartment that Mayers shared with twenty-five-year-old Danny Lambert. By the time the two arrived, Lambert was snoring in his bedroom, sleeping off a night of drinking. Harris and Mayers settled into the living room, but Mayers testified that after a few drinks and some cocaine, Harris made very aggressive sexual advances.

Mayers admitted that he had a drug habit, but he would not prostitute himself as a way of reimbursing Harris for the cocaine. An argument followed that quickly grew into a physical altercation, where Mayers struck Harris over the head "once or twice" with a baseball bat that had been in the apartment. He claimed it was self-defence.

Mayers then went to Lambert's room and shook him awake. He said Lambert then joined him in clubbing Harris about twenty times, with blows so hard the bat broke. This went against the testimony of Lambert, who said Mayers woke him in a panic, and then forced him to help dispose of the body that had already been beaten.

Mayers claimed that the two of them stripped Harris of his bloody clothing, wrapped him in blankets, and took him down to his car where they stuffed him in the trunk. They drove to Denman Street where they dumped Harris's bloody clothes in a trash can, and then on to Lost Lagoon where they abandoned the car along the side of North Lagoon Drive.

Afterward, they returned to the Bidwell Street apartment to clean up and wash the blood off themselves. Lambert testified that Mayers said, "I sure hope he's dead. I don't want him coming back to get me."

During the four days of court testimony, Harris, though the victim, was as much on trial as Mayers. The jury was told that Harris had been convicted in 1978 for living off the avails of prostitution and keeping a common bawdy house, and that the charges involved both male and female sex workers in the West End. They were also told that Harris preferred to have sex with young men and frequently used violence to get what he wanted.

James Islaub, a witness for the defence who had been the controller of the U-Frame-It company, stated in court that Hal Keller had paid Harris "at least

$4,500 a month" to procure boys for Keller's sexual habits, and that Harris used to boast about using violence "to keep the men and women in line—those working for him on the street."[28]

Austin Cullen, the Crown prosecutor in the case, argued that much of Mayers's testimony blaming Lambert was not believable. In his final arguments, he stated the jury was faced with a situation of "two men in a room with a dead body and each is pointing the finger at the other."

On April 22, 1986, a BC Supreme Court jury found Mayers guilty—not of second-degree murder but of the lesser charge of manslaughter, and sentenced him to four years in prison. The jury convicted on the lesser charge because Mayers said Harris had made aggressive sexual advances, so Mayers's actions were partially justified on the basis of self-defence.

The case had much in common with the legal strategy apparent in the "Bachelor Murders" of Eddie Beresford, Charles Chatten, and Robert White in the West End in the late 1950s, which was eventually put into common practice in the 1970s and '80s as the "gay panic" or "homosexual advance" defence. Defendants accused of murder claim to have committed the crime in a state of temporary insanity, in response to unwanted same-sex advances that were so offensive or frightening that they were provoked into reacting with violence. If Mayers had a different motive from what he stated at trial, we may never know.

Staff sergeant Rich Rollins was surprised that the court didn't accept the weightier charge of second-degree murder. The autopsy reports that still sit in the VPD homicide file, too graphic for publication, show the blows from the bat left deep head wounds. Combined with the evidence of cast-off bloodstain patterns at the Bidwell Street apartment, it's clear that Harris met an extremely violent end. "This wasn't a case where Mayers had hit him with a couple of glancing blows to keep him at bay," Rollins says. "That was Babe Ruth shit."

During the trial Mayers portrayed himself as a straight man preyed upon by Harris. This surprised those who knew Mayers as gay. Kevin Dale McKeown, a journalist who at nineteen became Vancouver's first out gay columnist in 1970, writing for the *Georgia Straight*, was once in a relationship with Mayers. He first met him at the Ambassador Hotel pub.

[28] Phil Needham, "Gay Pimp's Killer Found Guilty of Manslaughter," *Vancouver Sun*, April 23, 1986, 10.

"He talked a mile a minute," says McKeown. "He was one of those guys on the make and always working the angles, but he was charming and gregarious and told great stories. I liked him." The two moved in together for a period before Mayers was picked up for an assault in West Vancouver in the late 1970s. McKeown lost touch with Mayers after that.

"I was never really friends with Wayne [Harris], but everyone in the West End knew him," McKeown recalls. "People didn't think fondly of him. If he could use you, he was friendly, but if he couldn't see a use for you, he ignored you. We didn't have a lot of pimps in town who dealt with the boys. To have somebody who was actively pimping—he stood out that way."

McKeown recalls that a rumour circulated in the West End that Harris's murder was a targeted killing—revenge for Harris's rape of an adolescent boy who had been a friend of Mayers. But "I don't think that's true," McKeown says. "Clearly, cocaine was involved, and the expectation of sex that came with it. [Coke] was almost more common than pot back then. I saw Neall after he got out of jail when he showed up unexpectedly at my place on a visit to Vancouver, but we never discussed it or talked about it."

Mayers proved particularly elusive in subsequent years. After he served his four-year sentence, Mayers went to live in the Las Vegas area, where he had family. In 1992, he was involved in an armed robbery of a warehouse there and was later arrested. On Halloween night 1997, he and an accomplice robbed a Las Vegas bar. He was arrested days later but fled Nevada before he could be tried for the crime. Mayers showed up back in Vancouver in January 1998 on one of those "unexpected visits" that McKeown had received. While in BC, he was arrested and convicted for armed robberies he did in Victoria and Vancouver and served a five-year sentence. When that prison term was complete, he finally returned to Las Vegas in 2012 to face trial for the 1997 robbery. Nevada Department of Corrections records state that Mayers was released from prison in 2018, but his whereabouts today, despite considerable efforts by the author to track him down, are unknown. During his Las Vegas trial, he presented a false social security number and a false driver's licence number. If Neall Mayers is still alive in 2021, he would be sixty.

After Mayers was convicted in 1986 for manslaughter, public interest in the details of Wayne Harris's murder waned. For Staff Sergeant Rich Rollins, though, many questions about the investigation remained.

Mayers had taken a silver chain off Harris's neck before he dumped the car in Stanley Park. During the trial, Mayers claimed that taking the necklace was an act of faith, not theft. "I saw the crucifix gleaming at me, and I didn't think a person of evil should have something like that," he said, testifying that he later passed it along to a man named Randy Turner, who Mayers spoke to before he fled the country.

The necklace has a backstory. Constantine "Tyke" Thodos purchased it as a gift for Harris. The Thodos family operated the legendary seafood restaurant the Only on Hastings Street. Although it's unclear how Harris and Thodos knew each other, Harris had given $50,000 of his personal injury settlement to Thodos to invest on his behalf. What happened to the money that Thodos had invested for Harris is unknown. Thodos died in 2011.

The necklace would again pass hands, when Turner gave it to a chain-smoking, fifty-year-old Roman Catholic priest and, coincidentally enough, friend of Wayne Harris's, Father Alfred Sasso.

"That there was a connection with the archdiocese was just another element of how strange and bizarre this case got," says Rollins. "There was just so much fallout. Just when it couldn't get more bizarre, it did—we had a priest involved."

Sasso had first been ordained in 1965 at the Diocese of London, Ontario, where in 1980 he pleaded guilty to three counts of gross indecency involving three youths, one a former altar boy. His sentence seemed appallingly short: just three months—a month for each youth, with two years' probation. More appalling: after his sentence, in 1981, Sasso was transferred to the Archdiocese of Vancouver and served at St. Patrick's Roman Catholic Parish.

The investigation into Sasso's connection to Mayers revealed that the priest was paying rent for an apartment occupied by three teenage boys who had been procured by Wayne Harris. When Rollins called Sasso at St. Patrick's, Sasso claimed he was busy and couldn't meet to answer questions about Mayers. But Rollins told him it would be better if he came down to the police station, rather than having a homicide detective come knocking on his door at the church. Sasso said he'd come down to the station immediately.

"He broke down in tears during the interview," Rollins recalls. Sasso confessed to police that he usually visited the apartment on a Friday or Saturday night to have sex with the underage teens there and would always be back at St. Patrick's for Sunday services. "He wept like a kid after he spilled the beans. 'What do I do!?' he said. Well, I was disgusted with him. All I could tell him was, 'It's between you and your god.'"

Detective Doug Hardman, who had played a lead role in the early weeks of the Mayers investigation, recalls Sasso's confession. "We let him go and went to a prosecutor about what we'd learned. [The prosecutor] happened to be a good Catholic. The next day we learned Sasso had moved to Hawaii. It was that quick. I tracked Sasso down and called him, and he said he wasn't coming back. We could never pin things on that prosecutor, or that he had let somebody at the diocese know that Sasso was being looked at, but we were shocked and angered by it all and that it had gone that way."

That the case left some questions and crimes unanswered for was a particularly bitter pill for Hardman, who had been on the vice squad in the late 1970s and close to the Harris-Keller investigation when the telephone wiretaps were executed on Harris. "Wayne Harris was a really bad guy. He was raping these kids. It was awful stuff. I guess Wayne paid the price in the end, while others— too many—seemed to never answer for what they did."

Father Sasso was never brought to trial. He would eventually return to Ontario, where he served as a counsellor in a drug recovery treatment home. He died in 1991.

In the end, the most significant questions that were left unanswered with the murder of Wayne Harris were about the wider network he'd been involved in. Just who were the chicken hawks who had paid Harris to bring young hustlers to them? Mayers's killing of Harris seemed to make sure those names unearthed in Bader and Robson's original investigation would remain secret. Beyond Hal Keller, who had been involved, would any names from the Keller suicide and the Harris murder investigations be revealed? And were any of them still walking free today?

CHAPTER 11

Compromised

The death of Wayne Harris occurred just before the demise of the West End sex trade itself. On July 4, 1984, two months after Harris was killed, an injunction filed by BC Attorney General Brian Smith, and granted by BC Supreme Court Chief Justice Allan McEachern, effectively outlawed all sex work west of Burrard Street. McEachern called the situation of street sex work in the West End an "urban tragedy" and threatened that anyone arrested for violating the order would face contempt of court charges for which there were no set penalties. The chief justice used harsh words in his assessment: "Those who would defile our city should understand they can be subject to not only criminal law but also to common law. Public nuisance for the purposes of prostitution has gone on too long in this city." The injunction was strict in its interpretation of loitering or any behaviour that could be broadly defined as prostitution.

While sex workers were vehemently and vocally opposed, there was overwhelming support for the new ruling in the local media and among local residents who noticed an immediate change in the neighbourhood the following day. Even police noticed the difference. Constable Al Arsenault, who had joined the VPD in 1979 and been working in a juvenile offender division, recounts, "I was in and out of the West End a fair bit back then, and I'll never forget when the injunction came through. I thought the john traffic of those cruising for hookers back then was just a quarter of the local traffic, along with the lookie-loos who just used to drive around to watch the sex trade workers or make noise. But the day after the injunction, I couldn't believe the difference it made and how much less vehicle traffic there was. You could shoot a cannon down Davie Street and not hit anybody."

In many ways the injunction had predictable results. West End sex workers were pushed east of Granville Street along Seymour and Richards Streets and into the Mount Pleasant neighbourhood. Many would later criticize the injunction for forcing sex workers into more dangerous areas of the city, like the Downtown Eastside. Male prostitutes eventually migrated to the downtown district of Yaletown, to a one-block stretch of Homer Street between Davie and Drake. The district had for decades been an industrial area until condominium towers began to replace the old warehouses. But the street remained a stroll for young male hustlers until the early 2000s, when increasing residential development finally pushed them out. Sex workers fought the police for years, but they couldn't beat the strata committees and gentrification.

Constable Arsenault worked most of his policing career in the Downtown Eastside, where he saw the long-term results of the injunction that forced sex workers out of the West End. "The sex trade workers eventually went east, migrated down to the Downtown Eastside, which was worse for them of course," he says. "There was already prostitution happening around there, but there wasn't the kiddie stroll, which showed up after that. A whole new set of problems started to hit the skids after that."

Now that sex workers were evicted from the West End, and both Hal Keller and Wayne Harris were dead, it seemed there was little police interest in pursuing others named as clients of Harris who bought sex with underage youths. Yet there was one final opportunity for Vancouver police to expose this dark period in Vancouver's history and reveal a greater network of criminal activity, though in the end that, too, would come crashing down and be discredited before the truth could be revealed. This was the controversial case of John Michael Lewis and the notorious "Chicken Book," all but forgotten today, though for a time in the mid-1980s it was front-page news in Vancouver.

On July 27, 1982, acting on an anonymous tip, Vancouver vice squad detective George Kristensen, aided by two other police officers, raided the Cornwall Avenue home of thirty-four-year-old of John Lewis, a US citizen who worked in tourism and had been living in Vancouver since 1977. The anonymous caller told Kristensen that he would find inside Lewis's home a cache of drugs and very questionable pornography.

Although police discovered only a small amount of marijuana in the raid, they also confiscated two photo albums and an address book—the aforementioned Chicken Book that contained the names of Lewis's purported victims, as well as hundreds of everyday contacts, making it difficult to determine who was who.

The photo albums were filled with pictures of naked young men, many of whom appeared underaged. Questioning of Lewis revealed he had worked as a tour guide and recruited adolescents he'd met on trips to model for him in

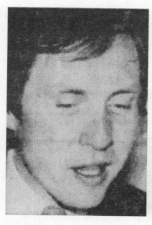

Police deny sex list links

The Los Angeles police department now denies it has any information or evidence "regarding any involvement of any Canadian official, including members of Parliament, being involved in any criminal activity."

Commander William Booth, head of the LAPD's press relations department, also said in a statement: "Any report attributing such knowledge to any member of this department is er-

Brambles and Bennett spoke to Sun on Friday.

Booth's statement was issued at p.m. Saturday and states in full: " Los Angeles police department has information and no evidence regard any involvement of any Canadian cial, including members of Parliam being involved in any criminal activ

"Any report attributing such kno edge to any member of this departm

John Michael Lewis in 1987.

photographs. In a follow-up search of the home, police found a locker full of thousands more photographs that, like the albums, included the dates of when the photographs had been taken as well as the names and ages of the young men.

After Kristensen performed the raid on Lewis's home, he was contacted by a Los Angeles police officer named Mike Brambles. Brambles was part of a special division of the LAPD vice squad that was established to investigate suspicions of child prostitution in LA. In 1980, Brambles's first major case involved Don Henley, drummer and singer for the rock band The Eagles, who was arrested for contributing to the delinquency of a minor when a sixteen-year-old female sex worker was found naked and high at his home.

In 1982, Brambles picked up a teenage runaway on suspected drug charges. When the runaway named Lewis in Vancouver as a contact, Brambles thought he'd uncovered a larger network of human trafficking along the West Coast. That's when Brambles and Kristensen started collaborating on the case. Kristensen and his partner, Del Blanchard, were able to track down many of the youths Lewis had photographed, and eventually charges were filed against Lewis in 1983. But the case would never go to trial. Lewis later said that due to the pressure of the investigation, and his lawyer having advised him to not fight the charges, he pleaded guilty to the oral sex and sodomy charges involving two youths ages fifteen and sixteen. Lewis was sentenced to six months in Oakalla Prison.

Meanwhile, Brambles had requested Lewis's photos which had been taken in the US, to see if any charges could be prosecuted in California. Kristensen sent copies of the photos and the address book. On August 26, 1983, Brambles held a press conference in LA where he announced that he had broken an international pornography and sexual exploitation ring that involved minors, as well as "prominent Canadians," including two politicians.

The VPD contradicted Brambles's claims, saying that police wouldn't confirm the existence of any child porn ring involving politicians. LAPD Commander William Booth retracted Brambles's statement, saying it had been erroneous. Brambles was not reprimanded. But by then the rumour mill couldn't be stopped, and some politicians were wrongly suspected.

Meanwhile, in 1984, after his conviction, Lewis had remarkably managed to rehabilitate his public image. With his connections to the tourism industry, he obtained a seat on the prestigious Vancouver Centennial Commission, which was involved in the planning of the 1986 centennial celebration in partnership with the Expo 86 world's fair. However, when the local media learned that a convicted sex offender was on the commission, the public outcry forced Lewis to resign. The police might not have convicted him for more crimes, but his public image was ruined, and he would be hounded out of the city.

In 1987, Lewis sued to have his photo albums and address book returned. The infamous Chicken Book was finally released. Lewis invited *Vancouver Sun* journalist Terry Glavin to review the material, and in an email to me, Glavin reported that it was nothing more than a simple, innocuous address book—there was no story. Had the police truly jumped to conclusions so egregiously?

Worse still, the case lost further credibility when the LAPD's Mike Brambles, once the department's star investigator, was arrested in 1994 on twenty-six charges including armed robbery and rape. He was sentenced to 102 years in prison but was released in 2020.

Afterward, just about anything Brambles had touched as an investigator was viewed as suspect, in particular the Lewis investigation.

In early 1998, Lewis was admitted to St. Paul's Hospital suffering from pneumonia related to AIDS, which he later died from. Lewis's fall from the heights of the Vancouver tourist and business world was charted by several columnists and writers at the time, arguing that police had been motivated by the homophobia of the time to harass Lewis and destroy his reputation—and life. Questions arose about just how much of the case had been speculation. One perspective was that because so few victims had ever filed a complaint against him, if they were willing participants, what was the problem? Though the truth was several were underage and many would have been coerced.

Public opinion at the time wasn't helped by the fact that the Vancouver vice squad—in particular Detective George Kristensen, who had been one of the main investigators—refused to comment or give interviews on the matter. But local media who were critical of the way the police handled the case didn't know the real story behind Lewis. Almost forty years after the Chicken Book story broke, Kristensen spoke for the first time.

"When I first interviewed John, he tried to pass it all off that he had this one little vice of photography, but it was harmless," Kristensen says today, at age seventy-three, having retired from the VPD in 2002. "The truth is, we uncovered so much stuff, but so much of it never came out. I remember going through those photo and address books—we found about twenty or thirty youths from Vancouver that we tracked down to interview. Lewis's target age range was about ten to sixteen or seventeen, and he really ruined the lives of a lot of these kids—most wouldn't talk or file a complaint. They were very intimidated."

Kristensen learned in interviews with those whom Lewis had photographed and molested that he had rented a trailer in Squamish, a town just north of Vancouver, and he'd regularly invited friends there. Wiretap information revealed that Lewis's friends brought youths to these parties in Squamish, much like the parties that Gord Bader and Al Robson had surveilled at Hal Keller's home in Point Grey.

Police learned from the wiretap that Lewis was selling the photographs and showing the photo albums to other predators he socialized with so they could choose who Lewis brought to a party for them.

"In those days, possession of child pornography wasn't an offence. It's remarkable to look back now and think of that," Kristensen says. "But part of the problem was the physical evidence of the photos we had. There wasn't much we could do with it."

In turn, when police showed up with questions, some of the parents of these minors had no idea what had happened to their children. Kristensen recalls one youth who was a runaway Lewis had found and groomed. By the time investigators caught up with him, the teenager was back with his family, and his parents had been unaware of anything untoward happening to him.

And what about the Chicken Book, which journalist Terry Glavin had reported was merely an ordinary address book?

"A good sex scandal never dies," Kristensen says. There was a fear that if the greater truth came out, it would cause far worse trouble. "During the investigation we got a new superintendent, and he thought there was something that would bite him in the ass one day, so the photo albums and address book got locked up, and the investigation went no further. We were given a written order not to show any sensitive faces or pictures from the photo album."

Kristensen asserts that what Glavin saw was in fact the address book with some names removed—names that he would have recognized. But Kristensen alleges it wasn't Vancouver police who altered the book but Lewis who removed pages and contacts before Glavin saw it.

Today, Glavin does not recall whether he noticed any obvious alterations or deletions in the book, or if Lewis would have had an opportunity to alter the book before it reached his hands.

However, Glavin never saw the photo albums, which contained the most damning material, Kristensen says, and justified the investigation in the first place. "Somewhere along the line, the address book was termed 'the chicken book' when we had always considered the photo albums to be that," Glavin says. "So it's no surprise that people thought the investigation went nowhere. The media was looking at the wrong thing."

After two years in the vice squad, Kristensen wrote a report about the Lewis investigation before he was promoted to another division. In it, Kristensen noted that it was the first time in his experience that the VPD had seen "an organized group of child molesters working together in Vancouver."

But Kristensen was disappointed by the reaction to his report. "Nobody seemed to do anything about it. The Crown counsel at that time didn't seem interested in prosecuting anybody. They just told us, 'See if you can run him out of town.' Those were the exact words they said ... In those days, if you came to them with an impaired driving charge, or shoplifting, it was 'Glad to see ya,' but if you presented them with a conspiracy file, it felt like they just dove under the table. It was considered that conspiracy cases like that burned up too many man-hours with the potential of nothing coming from it. Just getting the wiretap authorization on that case was a journey in itself. I don't think it's that way now, but it sure was then. The child pornography laws weren't as strict then, so maybe they just didn't think they could make charges stick."

The names of those who were in contact with Wayne Harris or John Lewis about sex with underage youths, whether listed in address books or heard on police wiretaps, were not investigated further by Vancouver police, until a July 2005 VPD report that covered several investigations over the course of decades was published within the department.

The report, titled "Review of Forty Years of Vancouver Police Department Records into an Organized Ring of Sexual Predators Targeting 'At Risk' Male Youth and Vancouver Police Department Purging Practices," spelled out for the first time the full extent of investigations that connected the Harris and Lewis cases, and presented suspects and persons of interest still alive at the time of publication whom investigators strongly thought warranted further review.

The report, which was distributed at the highest levels of the VPD, presented a series of startling allegations, asserting that "an organized group of influential men" operating in Vancouver have been sexually assaulting young men since the late 1960s.[29]

The report called the wiretap on Hal Keller as part of the "U-Frame-It" investigation conducted by Bader and Robson and vice squad members foundational, and observed that some clients of Wayne Harris were later associates of John Lewis, specifically for the purposes of meeting underage youths for child sexual exploitation.

As bold as the allegations are in the report, there is also the document's greatest weakness to consider—the quality and availability of the evidence.

Much of the original evidence gathered on the suspects from the Wayne Harris, Hal Keller, and John Lewis investigations had been shredded and destroyed as part of VPD purging practices, which routinely destroy material on old cases that didn't result in convictions or have to do with major crime cases. Although Hal Keller's open suicide file and Wayne Harris's murder file remain in police archives, the reports, wiretaps, and surveillance information that didn't result in further charges, arrests, or convictions were all eventually purged and destroyed after twenty-five to thirty years in accordance with common practice.

The 2005 report states, "When faced with a forty-year police data review it became clear that the Vancouver Police Department's past and present record keeping policy caused the destruction of most of the original police reports and evidence." Instead, much of the evidence in the report was gathered by individual investigators who, remarkably, in many cases kept personal copies of the files, photographs, complaints, and reports, which were supported by their own memories of the time. However, the quality and accuracy of the information in those files would likely come under scrutiny in court. And in the end, there seemed to be no appetite among police superintendents or chief inspectors, or any actions by Crown counsel, to pursue the alleged criminal activity that detectives in the street had uncovered.

---

[29] Jim Scott and Jennifer Keyes, "Review of Forty Years of Vancouver Police Department Records into an Organized Ring of Sexual Predators Targeting 'At Risk' Male Youth and Vancouver Police Department Purging Practices," unpublished report, July 2005.

"The department itself was always more concerned with street stuff back then," says one retired VPD member. "If there was a big name involved, as much as it could be a significant investigation, there was a fear if you got it wrong, it could come back to bite you and ruin your career. So they went after street stuff. Easy arrests. I don't think it's like that now—I hope it's not. But there were a lot of people then higher up who didn't want to rock the boat."

The 1970s and early '80s in the West End was one of the most turbulent periods in the history of the city. At no time before or since did so many disparate groups, trends, and forces come together in the evolution of one neighbourhood in a process that also summoned such a volatile response from residents and law enforcement who tried everything in their power to control—often misguidedly—its crime issues.

The era ushered in a change in local politics. Despite the 1984 court injunction that ended street sex work in the West End, the old brand of public morals politicians that had been a constant presence in municipal government for decades would no longer hold sway. Public perception of the LGBTQ+ community is markedly different from those years and even celebrated today. Although prejudice hasn't disappeared from the city, its citizens are markedly more inclusive now.

That we no longer wrestle with some of the conservative and repressive attitudes that divided Vancouver so strongly in the 1970s and '80s is a change for the better.

Epilogue

Vancouver's West End has changed immeasurably since the 1970s and '80s, when it was the place where sex workers, hustlers, and johns drew so much attention from the Vancouver vice squad. Many of the businesses on Davie Street have changed, though the original buildings remain, leaving the street as a kind of time capsule. But while it may not look so different, the neighbourhood is undergoing foundational transformation.

"Vancouver was very provincial in those days," recalls Andre Tardif, who arrived in Vancouver as a hitchhiking hustler in the 1970s and landed at the Taurus bathhouse. "It felt like a smaller town, where everybody knew one another. That's not a bad thing, but it's changed. And the West End is a lot different. Now there all these condos on Davie Street that weren't around in the seventies."

The Taurus is gone now, too. The Bon Accord Hotel burned down in a fire on the night of Valentine's Day 1992. A fifty-four-storey condo tower called Burrard Place will stand where the Taurus once was, and it's likely the new residents of the building, from the ground floor to the top multi-million-dollar penthouse, will have no idea of the diversions that once played out nightly in the steam-filled cubicles that formerly stood in its place.

The deadly wrecking ball of AIDS had already begun to do its damage in the West End by the time Taurus burned down. With the West End home to so many gay men by the 1990s, the neighbourhood experienced the wrath of the disease more explicitly than others. Many survivors of the period today can cite a litany of friends and lovers lost. The straight community in the West End was also affected by the tragedy of their neighbours dying at an alarming rate—many recall acquaintances, or just those who had been familiar faces for years, simply vanishing. The ripple effect that the AIDS epidemic had on the city has never been fully appreciated.

"Not enough has been made about how the decimation of the gay demographic affected the arts and culture of the city," says David Hawkes, West End resident and former DJ at the Luv-a-Fair nightclub on Seymour Street. "So many of the gay residents in the West End, who were dual income, with no kids, were patrons or ticket buyers to shows and events, or ran their own little shops. It added so much to the city." David is now one of the operators of the Hollywood Theatre and has witnessed seismic changes in the culture and demographics of the city over the years. "This happened in cities all over the world, of course, but it was more dramatic, I think, in Vancouver, because of our population, and because so many people who were a part of that arts and culture scene lived in the West End."

Despite the terrible impact of AIDS in those years, the West End has very much survived as the city's "gaybourhood." In part because of greater contemporary acceptance of the LGBTQ+ community, many younger residents of the area may not know the history of the gay pioneers who began businesses and nightclubs and made the West End their home. As time goes by, the geographical location may have less immediate significance to the gay community—the safety of the neighbourhood or its connection to the community might not seem as relevant to younger gay people, who feel safe to live in any neighbourhood they wish. Moreover, as the West End is considered a favourable area to live in, younger gay residents, like many others their age regardless of sexual orientation, may find themselves priced out of the area due to steadily rising rental and real estate costs.

Even the need for gay bars, which have always played an important role in the social fabric of the LGBTQ+ community, has less importance to the younger generation, who can now meet up through social networking and dating apps on their mobile phones.

Things have changed within the police department as well.

The Vancouver police department formerly known as the vice squad became the Counter Exploitation Unit (CEU) in 2013. The unit now avoids targeting those who operate voluntarily as sex workers and instead goes after those who are exploited by "age or force."

Sergeant Glenn Burchart, who joined the VPD in 1999, has seen the changes for himself. Having spent four years in the Counter Exploitation Unit, he notes that police approach the sex trade very differently from the way they did during the turbulent years in the West End, when the main strategy was making arrests. "The department really doesn't go after sex workers now. There are very, very few arrests and convictions done on them these days. There are probably some abolitionists about sex work who don't approve of that, but we go after arresting pimps now," he says.

Technology has greatly changed the landscape as well. Burchart notes that street sex work as it was in the 1970s and '80s might be largely a thing of the past, as certain websites have become the new strolls—which don't go unmonitored by the CEU.

The West End Sex Workers Memorial is perhaps the only concrete recognition of the adversarial dynamic between law enforcement and sex workers back in those years, and at its 2016 unveiling, Vancouver police superintendent Michelle Davey apologized to sex workers on behalf of the VPD.

The memorial did not come without controversy, however. Supporters considered the period to be a "golden age" for street prostitution, when street sex workers could work without pimps, and argued that groups like Concerned Residents of the West End and the Shame the Johns campaign drove vulnerable sex workers into more dangerous situations and neighbourhoods, leading to many deaths, including those of the dozens of missing women, many of them Indigenous, in the Downtown Eastside murdered by serial killer Robert Pickton.

But proponents of this narrative have not gone uncriticized. Although some sex workers in the West End did not have pimps, this was hardly an absolute condition. And for all the proclamations that the period was the golden age of prostitution in Vancouver, there seems to be no sufficient response to questions of how and why the presence of underage sex workers went unchecked during that time.

A solution to the issues in the West End would have been to legalize sex work and establish an official red-light district where sex workers could operate safely, probably in an area that was less residentially dense as the West End, though still accessible. But in 1977, there was little broad support in Vancouver for such a proposal, and with current Vancouver property values, there might be even less now.

Not all relationships between the police and West End groups have improved with age since those years. In 2020, the Vancouver Pride Society, which organizes the annual Pride Parade, announced that all members of law enforcement were completely barred from the parade, following a 2017 decision that banned police in uniform from being present at the event. The decision had been motivated in part by Black Lives Matter Vancouver representatives and other members of the community who asserted, with reason given the turbulent relationship between the police and the Black community in the US in particular, that a visible police presence made them feel unsafe. While the decision had its support among members of the LGBTQ community and their allies, many long-time participants in the parade—especially those who can recall when the relationship between the police and the LGBTQ community was at a nadir in the 1970s—consider the active participation of the VPD in the parade to be a positive turning point. It remains to be seen whether the relationship between the Vancouver Pride Society and the VPD will improve in the coming years, or if the division, emblematic of a greater cultural divide, will persist.

Jim Maitland, who probably spent more time on the vice squad than any other detective over the years, and even returned to it after spending time in other departments, finally retired in 1995. When the author showed Maitland the 2005 VPD report on sexual predators, he was astounded that nothing from the cases that linked Wayne Harris and Hal Keller and others was followed up any further. "I'm just surprised nothing happened, or that nobody even decided more investigation should have been merited."

Gord Bader spent some years on the Emergency Response Team and firearms training before he retired from the VPD in 1998, at the rank of detective. He worked with several partners over the years, but it's his time with Al Robson that he recalls most fondly and vividly.

"Al was great. He was innovative. He doesn't think like everybody else," Bader says. "Everything was funny to him, of course—he'd make a joke out of things. That sense of humour allowed him, and I suppose me in a way, to cut through the bullshit and come to a good conclusion about something really quick."

Robson, who retired in 1995, has equal praise for Bader. "He was the best partner. He was older than me but strong as a bull. It was good teamwork. I hated to call in sick, because I knew I was going to miss out on something. That's what it was like. No matter what happened. Car accidents, dead people, it's not an easy job, but I saw things that other people wouldn't see." In a rare moment of introspection, he adds, "I guess I was made for it."

Robson spent much of his later police career in special squads or on the drug squad. Today he sees cannabis retail stores and dispensaries on the same streets that he used to bust people for marijuana possession on. "I look back on a lot of that as a waste of time now. How could you not? But that was just a small part of what I did, or what we—Gord and I—did together."

There is a sense among many officers who worked in the 1970s that attitudes have greatly changed compared to when they policed in their day—be it cannabis possession or sex work. The world is a much different place now.

But looking back at the Wayne Harris case in the summer of 1977, Bader and Robson believe today that they were on the right path. And even though they've been retired from the department for years, if the VPD ever needed their services again, and if the coffee was hot enough, they'd still be up for a night shift on surveillance to follow up on the next lead, find the next clue, and discover where an investigation might go next.

For years, the West End has been one of the most desirable neighbourhoods in the city. But the conflicted period the community went through not so long ago will be recalled as a real turning point in the West End and in the history of Vancouver. Regardless of changing times, gentrification, and criminal activity, the vibrant beating heart of the West End continues to pump life through the community today as it did then.

Acknowledgments

I am quite fortunate that the cast of colleagues and friends to whom I am indebted has changed little with my successive books. At Arsenal Pulp Press: Brian Lam, Robert Ballantyne, Cynara Geissler, and editors Derek Fairbridge and Shirarose Wilensky offered immensely valuable comments and suggestions and corrected some of my most egregious errors. Thanks to Jazmin Welch for some early attention to images, and tremendous appreciation to designer Lisa Eng-Lodge, who once again took to the task under time constraints and deadlines. The Arsenal team have appropriately reined me in as required, pushed me when needed, and perhaps trusted me against their better judgment over five books now, and I feel my work is better for it. A warm welcome to Catharine Chen and Jaiden Dembo, the newest members of the Arsenal team, who I hope to be fortunate enough to work with sometime down the road.

Vancouver Vice could not have been told without the benefit of a number of contacts within the retired Vancouver Police Department community who have continued to share stories and memories with me, both on and off the record. Their thoughts and opinions continue to help me understand, for better or worse, the nature of their vocation. My thanks to Al Arsenault, Trevor Black, Vern Campbell, Chris Graham, Doug Hardman, Bill Harkema, Brian Honeybourn, Toby Hinton, George Kristensen, Tim Laidler, Grant MacDonald, Glenn McDonald, Mike Porteous, Bob Rich, Rich Rollins, Noreen Waters, Les Yeo, and the number of anonymous former VPD officers I interviewed or corresponded with for the purposes of this book and who, in some cases, entrusted me with confidential material.

Of course, a special thanks to Gord Bader and Al Robson, who were patient with me during countless hours of conversation, telephone calls, and emails recalling events of over forty years ago. Mr Robson's unique humour made some difficult subject matter easier to digest, and Mr Bader's archived notebooks were a considerable resource of specific dates, which helped to lift the fog on the details and the timeline and to confirm orbiting takes and issues with other sources and newspaper records.

While they will likely blanch at being referred to as "elders" within the LGBTQ+ community, many details of this story benefit from the recollections of veterans of the West End who have witnessed its many changes and, in many cases, continue to live there. My great appreciation to Andre Tardif, Donn Hann, Kevin Dale McKeown, and the late Jamie Lee Hamilton. They might disagree with one another on some issues, but all of them provided colour and detail to the highlights and lowlights of the West End during those years. Many thanks to Gordon Price, not only for his insights as an urban planner into the formation of the West End (which greatly informed the history of the West End in Chapter 2), but also for granting me access to his archival materials and photographs of the neighbourhood.

In speaking with a number of long-time West End residents, I was surprised to learn how well some of them recalled Wayne Harris and his associates. Their memories, both positive and negative, helped me to outline him beyond the police and media reports.

I've often heard it suggested that authors—particularly academic and cultural historians—are prey to jealousies. On the contrary, I am constantly amazed by the generosity of those who work in the wider historical community in Vancouver and elsewhere in British Columbia. With that, my thanks to John Atkin, John Mackie, Bill Allman, Michael Gordon, Michael Kluckner, and the Belshaw Gang, especially Jason Vanderhill, Eve Lazarus, and Tom Carter. And my thanks also to academic sociologist Dr Becki Ross for her elaboration on her own work, which crosses over into local history, and on the foundation of the West End Sex Workers Memorial.

The City of Vancouver Archives is one of the city's great institutions. The 2019 acquisition of local historian Ron Dutton's gay and lesbian archives, personally collected over forty years, will continue to yield fascinating viewpoints decades into the future. This and the 2018 donation by the *Vancouver Sun* and the *Province* of their photo library of 1.6 million photos make the Vancouver Archives indispensable to authors, historians, and the curious alike. Many of the images in this book come from photos in the archive's possession, and I thank my stars for the photographers, living or dead, whose work documented a city before it took on the polish of more recent years. Thanks to Carolyn Soltau for her help sourcing many *Vancouver Sun* images, and head archivist Heather Gordon at the City of Vancouver Archives for sourcing some of the more recent images from their collection.

My deep gratitude to Sarah Wotherspoon and her colleagues at the Vancouver Police Information and Privacy Unit for handling the multiple Freedom of Information requests I filed. I fear that from now on, they may run when they see my name as petitioner on the form, knowing I'll likely send them down to the dusty, rarely visited shelves. I have always found the unit to be diligent and professional, even if what is forwarded to me is redacted more than I would prefer. I understand that the files they deal with can be difficult and that not all information can be available to the public yet, not even to a well-meaning historian.

So many thanks to Joe Average; Squire Barnes and all at Global BC; Kim Bolan; Gyles Brandreth; CBC Vancouver; Peter Chapman; CKNW Radio; Justice Austin Cullen; Danny Filippone; Will Woods and everyone at Forbidden Vancouver Walking Tours; the Friends of the Vancouver City Archives; Daniel Gawthrop; Marcus Gee; the *Georgia Straight*; Terry Glavin; Judge Thomas Gove; Sir Max Hastings; Heritage Vancouver; Sean Mawhinney and David Hawkes and everyone at the Hollywood Theatre; everyone at Live Nation British Columbia; Jason Manning; Kyla McDonal; Ros Oberlyn; Chief Constable Adam Palmer; Stan Persky; Laurence Rankin; Svend Robinson; Judge Valmond Romilly; the Royal Historical Society in the UK; Mark Schwartz; Professor Gary Sheffield; David Steverding and all at Odd Squad Productions; the Todd family; the Vancouver Historical Society; *Vancouver Is Awesome*; and the Vancouver Police Museum & Archives.

I wish to collectively thank those listed as interviewees in the Bibliography; they answered many of my questions and contributed much to making this book possible. While not all are quoted in the text, they all very much informed it. I've kept recordings of our chats on archive; they will likely help with future work.

My thanks to my many sources—from sex workers, customers, bartenders, bouncers, and West End residents new and old—who wished to remain anonymous.

aaronchapman.net

Bibliography

Books, Articles, and Reports

"Action against Bookstores Delayed for Appeal Outcome." *Province*, Jan. 19, 1966.

Anderson, Charlie. "Resident Loses All in Hotel Blaze." *Province*, Feb. 16, 1992.

"Bartender Killed in Violent Struggle." *Province*, Mar. 9, 1959.

"Bartender Slain in West End Suite." *Vancouver Sun*, Mar. 9, 1959.

"BC Court proceedings, Court file # C33807-01-D." Police file #98-14668/D.

"B.C. Man Puts Self Right in the Picture." *Province*, Mar. 1, 1978.

"Bitter Humour Flashes in Courtroom as Bookies, Officer Give Evidence." *Vancouver News-Herald*, Dec. 1, 1951.

"Black Book Bawd Gets 3 Months." *Vancouver Sun*, Dec. 10, 1952.

Blair, Richard and Moira Farrow. "Women Afraid to Go Out after Dark." *Vancouver Sun*, Sep. 17, 1969.

"Body Left in Trunk, Trial Told." *Vancouver Sun*, Apr. 15, 1986.

Bohn, Glenn. "Men of the Vice Squad Ride by Night, Armed with Bylaw." *Vancouver Sun*, Apr. 29, 1982.

"Call Girl Racket Big Business Here." *Vancouver Sun*, Feb. 17, 1961.

"Call Girl Ring Broken by Police." *Province*, Nov. 12, 1960.

"Cameron in Charge of Vice Squad." *Province*, Jun. 9, 1933.

Cassidy, Dan. "Wide-Open Prostitution Trade 'Threatening Tourist Business.'" *Vancouver Sun*, Jul. 7, 1980.

"City Call Girl Ring Exposed in Court." *Vancouver Sun*, Feb. 17, 1961.

"City Forms Special Squad to Fight Prostitution Rise." *Vancouver Sun*, Sep. 8, 1977.

"City Man Jailed on LSD Charge." *Vancouver Sun*, Jul. 20, 1966.

Cronshaw, Keith. "Mob Lurks in City Shadows." *Vancouver Sun*, Apr. 4, 1972.

"Davie Street Meet 'Was Not a Success.'" *Province*, Apr. 7, 1977.

"Davie Street Village." *Places That Matter*, Vancouver Heritage Foundation, n.d. placesthatmatter.ca/location/davie-street-village/. Accessed September 5, 2021.

Davis, Chuck. *The Greater Vancouver Book: An Urban Encyclopedia*. Surrey, BC: Linkman Press, 1997.

Davis, Chuck, ed. *The Vancouver Book*. North Vancouver: JJ Douglas Ltd, 1976.

"Dream Drug Grabbed in Wide-Awake Raid." *Vancouver Sun*, May 6, 1966.

"Extradited Man to Stand Trial." *Vancouver Sun*, Nov. 21, 1985.

"Five Charged with Prostitution." *Vancouver Sun*. Apr. 13, 1977.

Fotheringham, Allan. "Who Is Alex Dicimbriani?" *Vancouver Sun*, Apr. 24, 1974.

Francis, Daniel. *Red Light Neon: A History of Vancouver's Sex Trade*. Vancouver: Subway Books, 2006.

Gee, Marcus. "Boy Prostitutes Moving Onto Davie Street Corners." *Vancouver Province*, Aug. 13, 1977.

Gee, Marcus. "Vancouver's Homosexual 'Chicken Trade' Shocks City." *Vancouver Province*, Aug. 22, 1977.

Glavin, Terry. "Trial by the Book." *Vancouver Sun*, Aug. 29, 1987.

Glover, Randy. "Aldermen Ignore Brothel Warning, OK Steam Bath." *Vancouver Sun*, Oct. 26, 1977.

Greece, Paul. "Get Off the Road, Chum! There's a Sniper Up There!" *Ottawa Citizen*, Jul. 21, 1973.

Greenby, Mike. "Old, Young, Swinger or Loner, West End Story Runs Full Circle." *Vancouver Sun*, Oct. 29, 1969.

Hansen, Darah. "Staff to Assist Sex Trade Workers." *Vancouver Sun*, Jan. 30, 2013.

"Harried West End May Use Vigilantes." *Province*, Dec. 20, 1963.

Harwood, Holly. "Vigilantes to Hit Johns at Front Doors." *Province*, May 24, 1984.

Hobbs, Lisa. "Pretty Men with Sex for Sale Have an Out in Criminal Code." *Vancouver Sun*, Oct. 29, 1971.

Hunter, Don. "Odds-On, Baby." *Province*, Feb. 5th, 1977.

"In the West End." *Westender*, Jan. 5, 1984.

"Isobutyl Nitrite Is Prohibited." *Vancouver Sun*, Jan. 6, 2001.

Ivens, Andy. "Dicimbriani Ducks Jail on Sex Counts." *Province*, Dec. 7, 1997.

Jackson, Clive. "Hookers' Numbers Up, Competition Forces Rates Down." *Province*, May 23, 1978.

Johnson, Brian D. "Selling Sex on the Street." *Maclean's*, Apr. 16, 1984.

"Judge Warns Prostitutes, Procurers to Stay Away from Residential Areas." *Vancouver Sun*, Sep. 30, 1978.

Layton, Monique. "Prostitution in Vancouver, 1973–1975." Report to the BC Police Commission. Sep. 1975.

Lowman, John. *Regulating Sex: An Anthology of Commentaries on the Findings and Recommendations of the Badgley and Fraser Reports*. Burnaby: SFU Criminology, 1986.

Macdonald, Bruce. *Vancouver: A Visual History*. Vancouver: Talonbooks, 1992.

"Man Charged after Raid." *Vancouver Sun*, Dec. 23, 1975.

"Man Gets 4 Years." *Vancouver Sun*, Jun. 21, 1986.

"Many Vancouver Boys Acting as Male Prostitutes." *Vancouver Sun*. Aug. 17, 1977.

Mckenzie, Art. "New Life for Old Houses—West End Success Story." *Province*, Aug. 16, 1967.

Morgan, Keith. "Police Crack Child-Sex Ring." *Province*, Aug. 5, 1983.

"Mulligan Lists 'Vice Centres.'" *Vancouver Sun*, Mar. 20, 1947.

"Murder Trial Told Death Accidental." *Vancouver Sun*, Jun. 4, 1959.

"Murder Victim Told of Threats." *Vancouver Sun*, Jan. 16, 1959.

Needham, Phil. "Ex-Employee's Suit Bares Sexual Orgies." *Vancouver Sun*, Dec. 5, 1986.

Needham, Phil. "Gay Pimp's Killer Found Guilty of Manslaughter." *Vancouver Sun*, Apr. 23, 1986.

"New Theory Given in White Murder." *Vancouver Sun*, Mar. 14, 1959.

"Nine Killed on Highways During Holiday Weekend." *Vancouver Sun*, Aug. 2, 1977.

"No Proof Obscenity Corrupts." *Province*, Sep. 5, 1968.

Oake, George. "Sexual Supermarket—West End Vancouver's Bizarre Business Has Residents Fuming." *Calgary Herald*, Oct. 30, 1981.

Oberlyn, Ros. "Mapping Out the Markets Peddling Young Flesh." *Vancouver Sun*, Jul. 5, 1980.

Oberlyn, Ros. "'Sad Life' of a Chickenhawk." *Vancouver Sun*, Jul. 7, 1980.

"Obscenity Case: Sex, Crime, Rampant in Books." *Vancouver Sun*, Sep. 4, 1964.

"Obscenity Trial Delayed for Supreme Court Ruling." *Vancouver Sun*, Apr. 10, 1964.

"Over 200 Illegal 'Joints' Here in '46" *Vancouver Sun*, Mar. 20, 1947.

Persky, Stan. *The House That Jack Built: Mayor Jack Volrich and Vancouver Politics*. Vancouver: New Star Books, 1980.

"Perversion Racket Charged." *Vancouver Sun*, Jan. 16, 1964.

"Police Charge Six in Alleged Prostitute Ring." *Province*, Apr. 14, 1977.

"Police Deny Sex List Links." *Vancouver Sun*, Aug. 29, 1983.

"Police Dep't Buzzes Over Shakeup Talk." *Vancouver Sun*, Dec. 12, 1946.

"Police Hunt Sniper as 3 Hit in West End Shooting Spree." *Vancouver Sun*, Oct. 15, 1980.

"Police Officers Shifted." *Vancouver Sun*, Jan. 9, 1931.

"Police Protection Charge." *Vancouver Sun*, Oct. 12, 1933.

"Police Squads Seek Sniper in West End." *Province*, Jun. 1, 1973.

"Police Turn On Heat in Gastown." *Province*, Jul. 24, 1971.

Poulsen, Chuck. "B.C. Gamblers Watch Cards and Law Too." *Province*, Jul. 26, 1974.

Price, Gordon. "Original Greening: How the West End Went from Pavement to Plaza." *Viewpoint Vancouver*, Sep. 10, 2019, viewpointvancouver.ca/2019/09/10/original-greening-how-the-west-end-went-from-pavement-to-plaza/. Accessed August 11, 2021.

Pynn, Larry. "Ladies of the Evening Forced to Work the Afternoon Shift." *Vancouver Sun*, Jul. 9, 1979.

Queenan, Joe. "Scam Capital of the World." *Forbes*, May 29, 1989.

Robbins, Dennis. "The Faces of Our Youth." *Xtra! West*, Dec. 6, 2006.

Rose, Catherine. "Street Kings: The Dirty '30s and Vancouver's Unholy Trinity." In *Vancouver Confidential*, edited by John Belshaw. Vancouver: Anvil Press, 2014.

Sarti, Robert. "Traffic Diverters Irk Firemen." *Vancouver Sun*, Nov. 21, 1981.

Schaefer, Glen. "Hookers Laugh at Diverters." *Vancouver Sun*, Nov. 23, 1981.

Scott, Jim, and Jennifer Keyes. "Review of Forty Years of Vancouver Police Department Records into an Organized Ring of Sexual Predators Targeting 'At Risk' Male Youth and Vancouver Police Department Purging Practices." Unpublished report, Jul. 2005.

"Search for Slayer Hits Blank Wall." *Vancouver Sun*, Mar. 10, 1959.

"Second Stabbing Near St. Paul's." *Nanaimo Daily News*, Sep. 25, 1969.

"Sex in Baths. Tighter Control Sought." *Province*, Sep. 27, 1973.

Shillington, Stan. "High Rise Area Hard to Police." *Vancouver Sun*, Sep. 20, 1968.

"6 Held on Morals Charges." *Vancouver Sun*, Apr. 13, 1977.

"Some Steam Baths Have 'Boys for Rent.'" *Province*, Sep. 27, 1975.

St. Pierre, Paul. "Eat, Drink and Be Merry—It's Davie Street and 3 a.m." *Vancouver Sun*, Apr. 23, 1977.

"Street Mugging Victim 'Stabbed 18 Times.'" *Vancouver Sun*, Aug. 6, 1974.

Supreme Court of Canada. *Hutt v. the Queen*, [1978] 2 S.C.R. 476. decisions.scc-csc.ca/scc-csc/scc-csc/en/item/6076/index.do.

"Suspended Detectives Summoned." *Province*, Feb. 10, 1933.

Swan, Joe. *A Century of Service: The Vancouver Police, 1988–1986*. Vancouver: Vancouver Police Historical Society And Centennial Museum, 1986.

"Trial Ordered in Shotgun Incident." *Vancouver Sun*, Dec. 1, 1975.

Truelove, Graeme. *Svend Robinson: A Life in Politics*. Vancouver: New Star Books, 2013.

"$20,000 Reward Set in West End Killing." *Vancouver Sun*, Aug. 23, 1974.

Vickers, Yorke. "West End Sniper Convicted." *Vancouver Sun*, Feb. 21, 1981.

Volkart, Carol. "Prostitutes, Gays Clash with Residents." *Vancouver Sun*, Apr. 7, 1977.

"Volrich and the Vice Squad." *Victoria Times*, Mar. 26, 1977.

"West End Starts Unique Comeback." *Vancouver Sun*, Mar. 30, 1953.

"West End Streets Clear as Prostitutes Stay East." *Vancouver Sun*, Jul. 9, 1984.

White, Kayce. "Life Is Neat and the Money's Great for the Young Virgin from Pembroke." *Vancouver Sun*, Jul. 9, 1979.

"Young Boys 'Cost $10' in Baths." *Vancouver Sun*, Sep. 26, 1975.

Vancouver Police Department Case Files

FOI on VPD Case File #79-66689 "Sudden Death of Harold (Hal) Keller"—IPU 20-0478A.

FOI on VPD Case File #84-26812 WRH Homicide file—IPU 20-0478A.

FOI on VPD Case File #98-014668—Neall MAYERS—0401C Robbery with firearms file—IPU 20-0478A.

VPD Local Criminal Record #57746 for Wayne Robert HARRIS aka Robert Wayne HARRIS.

Interviewees

Arsenault, Al. Feb. 22, 2021.

Bader, Gordon. 2020–2021.

Becker, Brian. Apr. 8, 2020.

Black, Trevor. May 10, 2021.

Bligh, Kathy. Oct. 7, 2020.

Boston, Robert. Jun. 5, 2020.

Brail, Richard. Mar. 26, 2020.

Burchart, Glenn. Mar. 23, 2021.

Catterall, John. Jan. 3, 2020.

Chu, Jim. Oct. 29, 2020.

Clay, Jamie, Pearl Chow, and Lana and Barazzuol Chow. Nov. 2, 2020.

Dent, Bertram. Jul. 17, 2020.

Dixon, Paul. Apr. 1, 2020.

Dixon, Ted. Oct. 15, 2020.

Gee, Marcus. Apr. 27, 2020.

Gibson, David. Oct. 5, 2020.

Glavin, Terry. Jun. 9, 2018.

Gove, Thomas. Jun. 17, 2021.

Hann, Don. 2020–2021.

Harcourt, Mike. Oct. 23, 2020.

Hardman, Doug. Oct. 16, 2020.

Hawkes, David. Dec. 9, 2020.

Hurmuses, Gayle. Oct. 2, 2020.

Johnson, Bob. May 24, 2020

Joyce, Rob. Mar. 15, 2021.

Kearse, Ron. Oct. 2, 2020.

Kristensen, George. Mar. 2020.

Laidler, Tim. Apr. 15, 2020.

Lowman, John. May 19, 2021.

Lucas, Richard. Oct. 5, 2020.

Lys, Dean. Dec. 22, 2020.

MacDonald, Glenn. Jan. 30, 2020.

MacDonald, Grant. Jan. 23, 2020.

MacPherson, Guy. Oct. 9, 2020.

Maitland, Jim. Apr. 17, 2017.

McKeown, Kevin Dale. May 3, 2019.

Molnar, Eleanora. Oct. 2, 2020.

Oberlyn, Ros. Ap. 20, 2020.

Palmer, Adam. Mar. 22, 2021.

Parks Gord. Oct. 5, 2020.

Post, Pamela. Jul. 24, 2020.

Price, Gordon. Oct. 14, 2020.

Pruden, George. Mar. 3, 2019.

Rich, Bob. May 25, 2020.

Robbins, Dennis. Feb. 20, 2020.

Robinson, Art. Feb. 19, 2020.

Robson, Al. 2016–2021.

Rollins, Rich. Jan. 6, 2021.

Romilly, Valmond. Mar. 29, 2020.

Ross, Becki. May 14, 2021

Sarti, Doug. Oct. 2, 2020.

Schultz, Cathryn. Jun. 15, 2020

Smith, Brian. Nov. 23, 2020.

St. Louis, Maureen. Dec. 29, 2020.

Streit, John. Dec. 30, 2020.

Tardif, Andre. Sep. 25, 2020

Urchenko, Tom. Oct. 30, 2020.

Waddell, Ian. May 2, 2020.

Waters, Noreen. Apr. 13, 2020.

Winckler, Bruce. Jun. 16, 2020.

Yeo, Les. May 11, 2021.

Index

AARON CHAPMAN is a writer, historian, and musician. He is the author of *Vancouver after Dark: The Wild History of a City's Nightlife*, winner of the Bill Duthie Booksellers' Choice Award (BC and Yukon Book Prizes) in 2020; *The Last Gang in Town*, winner of the Canadian Historical Association's Clio Prize for BC in 2017; *Liquor, Lust, and the Law*, the story of Vancouver's Penthouse Nightclub, now available in a second edition; and *Live at the Commodore*, a history of the Commodore Ballroom that won the Bill Duthie Booksellers' Choice Award in 2015. A graduate of the University of British Columbia, in 2020, he was elected as a member of the Royal Historical Society. He lives in Vancouver.

Twitter: *@TheAaronChapman*